Jan 2020

CIVIL RIGHTS LEADERS

MALCOLM X

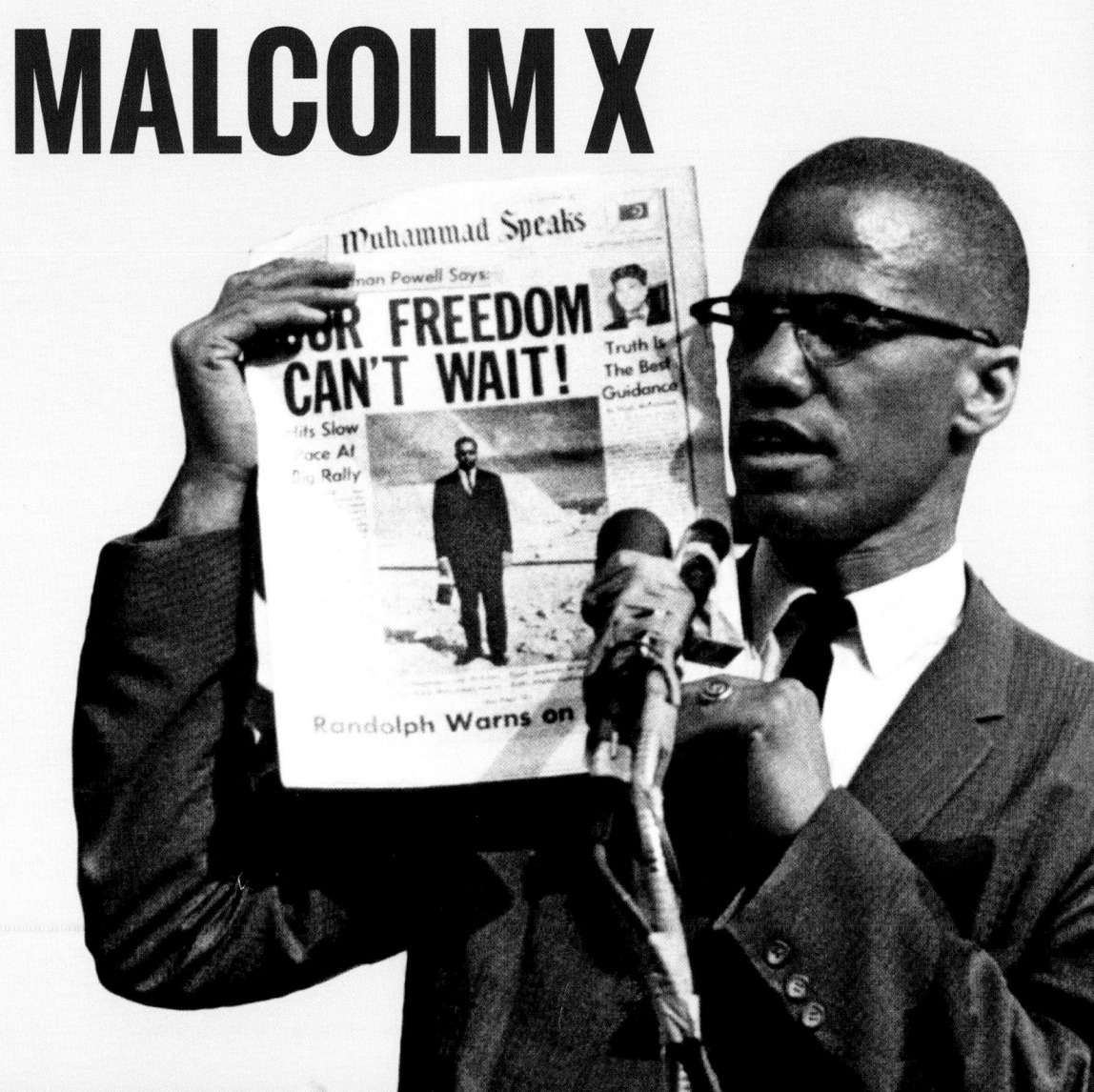

CIVIL RIGHTS LEADERS

Al Sharpton

Coretta Scott King

James Farmer

Jesse Jackson

Malcolm X

Martin Luther King Jr.

Mary McLeod Bethune

Rosa Parks

Thurgood Marshall

CIVIL RIGHTS LEADERS

MALCOLM X

Jillian Redmond

MASON CREST

Mason Crest
450 Parkway Drive, Suite D
Broomall, Pennsylvania 19008
(866) MCP-BOOK (toll-free)
www.masoncrest.com

© 2019 by Mason Crest, an imprint of National Highlights, Inc.
All rights reserved. No part of this publication may be reproduced or transmitted in any form or by any means, electronic or mechanical, including photocopying, recording, taping, or any information storage and retrieval system, without permission from the publisher.

Printed and bound in the United States of America.

CPSIA Compliance Information: Batch #CRL2018.
For further information, contact Mason Crest at 1-866-MCP-Book.

First printing
1 3 5 7 9 8 6 4 2

Library of Congress Cataloging-in-Publication Data on file at the Library of Congress.

ISBN: 978-1-4222-4007-6 (hc)
Civil Rights Leaders series ISBN: 978-1-4222-4002-1

Publisher's Note: Websites listed in this book were active at the time of publication. The publisher is not responsible for websites that have changed their address or discontinued operation since the date of publication. The publisher reviews and updates the websites each time the book is reprinted.

QR CODES AND LINKS TO THIRD-PARTY CONTENT
You may gain access to certain third-party content ("Third-Party Sites") by scanning and using the QR Codes that appear in this publication (the "QR Codes"). We do not operate or control in any respect any information, products, or services on such Third-Party Sites linked to by us via the QR Codes included in this publication, and we assume no responsibility for any materials you may access using the QR Codes. Your use of the QR Codes may be subject to terms, limitations, or restrictions set forth in the applicable terms of use or otherwise established by the owners of the Third-Party Sites. Our linking to such Third-Party Sites via the QR Codes does not imply an endorsement or sponsorship of such Third-Party Sites or the information, products, or services offered on or through the Third-Party Sites, nor does it imply an endorsement or sponsorship of this publication by the owners of such Third-Party Sites.

PHOTO CREDITS: Alamy: pg. 1; Library of Congress: pg. 6, 8, 13, 14, 18, 36, 42, 57, 62, 69, 71, 85, 90, 92, 93, 98, 102, 106, 118, 123; Shutterstock.com: pg. 11, 32, 48, 51, 65, 80, 114; Everett Historical: pg. 16, 21, 23, 24, 39, 40, 59; Boston Herald: pg. 17; National Archives: pg. 76, 82, 86; New York Daily News: pg. 110; United Nations Photo: pg. 117

TABLE OF CONTENTS

1. The Cities Are Burning. 7
2. A Challenging Childhood 17
3. Into the Underworld 33
4. Prison Epiphany 49
5. Nation of Islam. 63
6. The Leader of Temple Number Seven 77
7. Husband, Father, Fighter 91
8. Challenges and Threats 107
Further Reading 126
Internet Resources 126
Index. 127
About the Author 128

KEY ICONS TO LOOK FOR:

Words to Understand: These words with their easy-to-understand definitions will increase the reader's understanding of the text while building vocabulary skills.

Sidebars: This boxed material within the main text allows readers to build knowledge, gain insights, explore possibilities, and broaden their perspectives by weaving together additional information to provide realistic and holistic perspectives.

Educational Videos: Readers can view videos by scanning our QR codes, providing them with additional educational content to supplement the text. Examples include news coverage, moments in history, speeches, iconic sports moments and much more!

Text-Dependent Questions: These questions send the reader back to the text for more careful attention to the evidence presented there.

Research Projects: Readers are pointed toward areas of further inquiry connected to each chapter. Suggestions are provided for projects that encourage deeper research and analysis.

Series Glossary of Key Terms: This back-of-the book glossary contains terminology used throughout this series. Words found here increase the reader's ability to read and comprehend higher-level books and articles in this field.

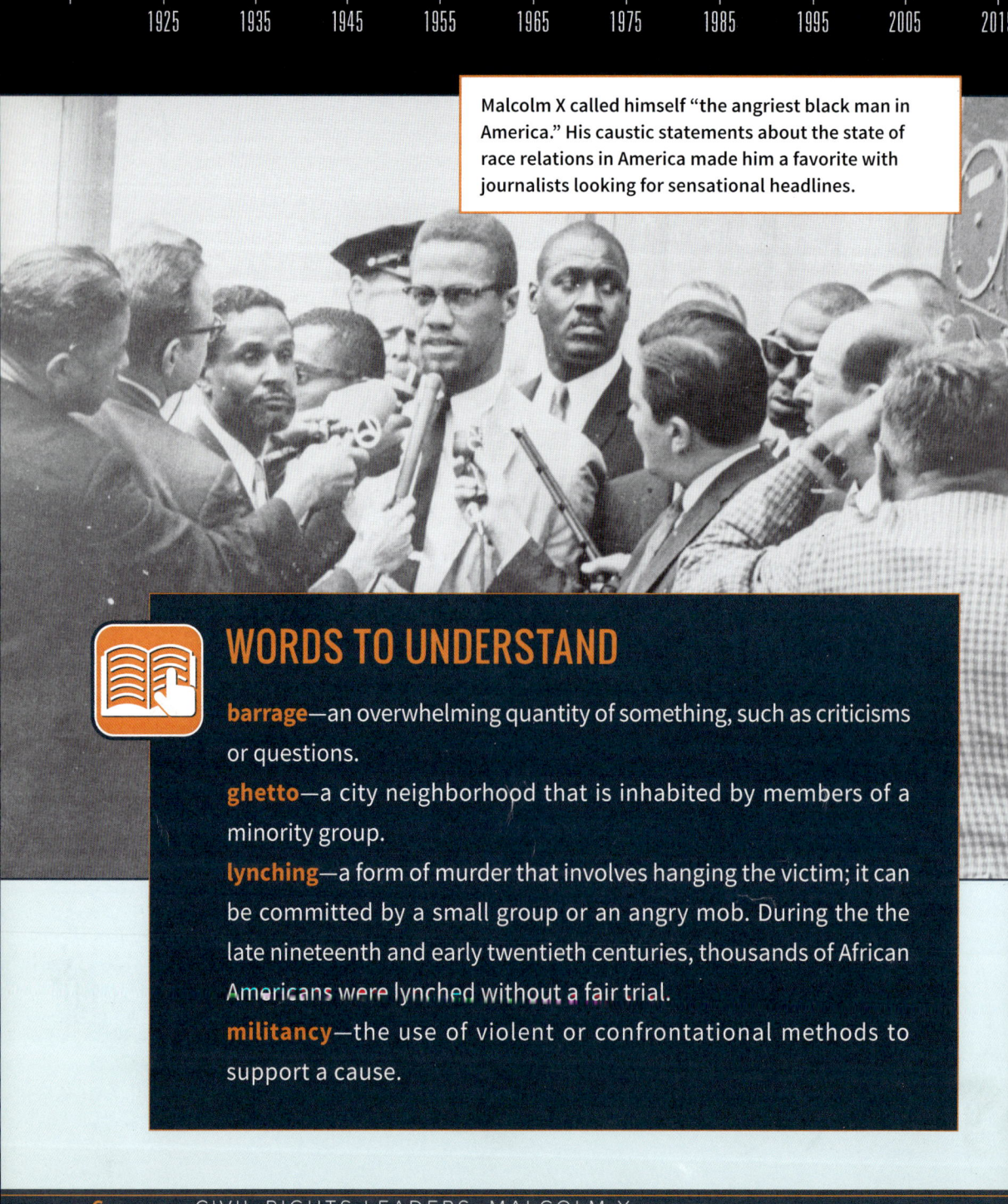

Malcolm X called himself "the angriest black man in America." His caustic statements about the state of race relations in America made him a favorite with journalists looking for sensational headlines.

WORDS TO UNDERSTAND

barrage—an overwhelming quantity of something, such as criticisms or questions.

ghetto—a city neighborhood that is inhabited by members of a minority group.

lynching—a form of murder that involves hanging the victim; it can be committed by a small group or an angry mob. During the the late nineteenth and early twentieth centuries, thousands of African Americans were lynched without a fair trial.

militancy—the use of violent or confrontational methods to support a cause.

CIVIL RIGHTS LEADERS: MALCOLM X

CHAPTER 1

THE CITIES ARE BURNING

On the afternoon of May 21, 1964, nearly 60 newspaper reporters crowded into the VIP lounge at Kennedy International Airport on the outskirts of New York City, anxiously awaiting the arrival of **militant** black leader Malcolm X. The journalists, most of whom were white and worked for the major New York newspapers, were worried about their approaching deadlines. Yet all of the reporters preferred to risk being late with their copy than leave without hearing what Malcolm X had to say upon his return from a tour of Africa and the Middle East.

The 39-year-old civil rights activist had been away from the United States for only five weeks, but during his brief absence racial relations had become even more strained. Many blacks were voicing their anger over how little progress had been made on the issue of civil rights. Many whites strongly opposed the few social reforms that were instituted to bring about greater racial equality.

Police and local black leaders had predicted that mounting racial tensions would lead to a summer of violence in the black **ghettos** of several major American cities.

Nowhere did this threat of violence loom greater than in New York, which boasted the largest black population in the nation. In fact, the city's police department had recently claimed to have uncovered a black vigilante group, the "Blood Brothers," that had been posing as a gun club. Their aim, according to the police, was to spill blood and incite violence.

Many people, including those in the media, were searching for clues as to what would happen next, and Malcolm X was thought to be an important resource. Noted for his willingness to approach controversial subjects that more moderate civil rights leaders usually avoided, he had gained the trust of America's urban blacks. He was not a man to mince words, and he was not afraid to hammer away with his demands for changes in American society.

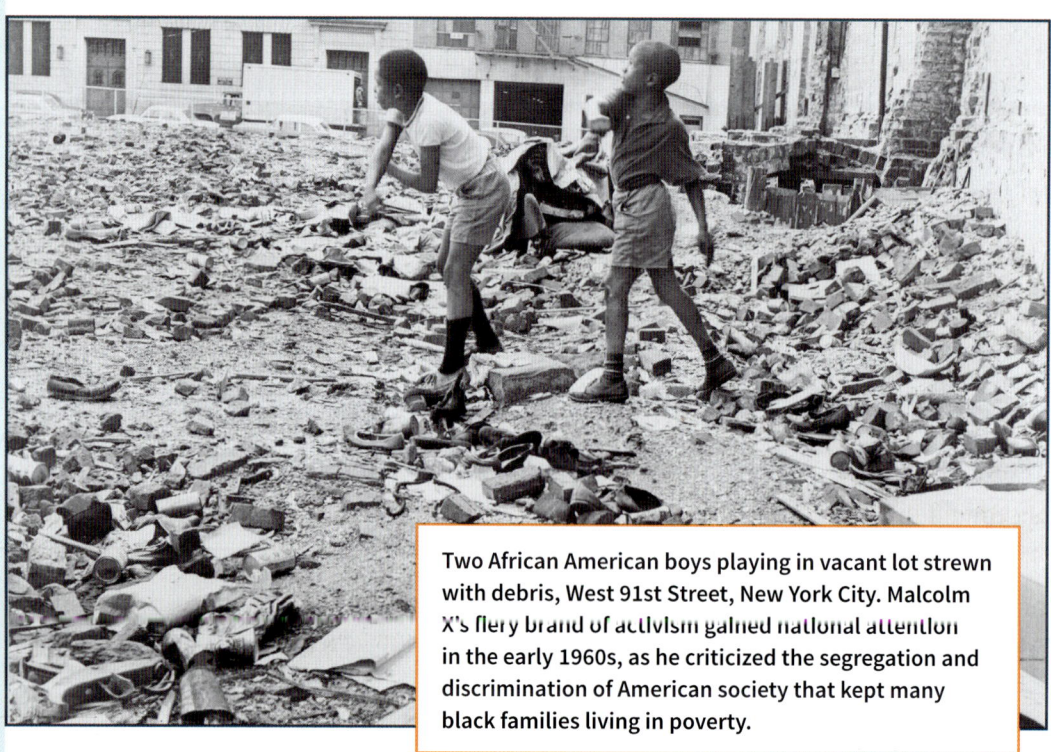

Two African American boys playing in vacant lot strewn with debris, West 91st Street, New York City. Malcolm X's fiery brand of activism gained national attention in the early 1960s, as he criticized the segregation and discrimination of American society that kept many black families living in poverty.

Malcolm X's ultimate goal was the liberation of black Americans from what he believed was a brutally oppressive, white-dominated power structure. While less revolutionary black leaders, especially the Reverend Martin Luther King, Jr., struggled to bring about greater racial integration in American society, Malcolm X repeatedly stated that the old order must be completely destroyed and replaced with new political and economic systems that allow blacks and whites to share power equally. Knowing how unlikely it was that the old structures would collapse, he often called upon black Americans to cut their ties with their country and found a separate nation. Yet as his flight from Algeria touched down at the airport, he was returning to a country that was still far from ready to accept his radical programs.

When Malcolm X emerged from the international arrivals gate, he was greeted by his wife and children and a group of his close associates. There was a sudden, excited bustling in the lounge area as the reporters caught sight of the tall, lean man with a wispy new beard. They flocked around him and unleashed a **barrage** of questions.

Only after Malcolm X seated himself at a nearby table and faced the reporters would he allow himself to be interviewed. He had become a master at using the media to publicize his political message, treating press sessions like a kind of game. The game was a serious one, though, for its object was the creation of a black political revolution in the United States.

The first question posed to Malcolm X was about the Blood Brothers, to whom he supposedly had ties. Indeed, he was the first black leader to have made a public statement calling for blacks to form gun clubs to protect themselves. If Malcolm X supported the Blood Brothers, one reporter asked, was he not "a teacher, a fomentor of violence?"

Malcolm X answered by pointing out what he believed were contradictions in the way the press—mainly the white press—wrote about the issue of self-defense in the case of racial attacks. It was considered normal for whites to buy guns for their self-defense, he said, but when blacks took up arms to protect themselves against

lynch mobs, it was viewed as a potentially dangerous situation. "I'm for justice," he told the reporters. "When the law fails to protect Negroes from whites' attacks, then those Negroes should use arms, if necessary, to defend themselves."

Another reporter wanted to know why Malcolm X always had to "stir up" blacks. It was a question that seemed almost ludicrous to Malcolm X, who spent most of his life among people whose poverty and misery had gone virtually unnoticed by much of white America. He wearily answered, "It takes no one to stir up the sociological dynamite that stems from unemployment, bad housing, and inferior education already in the ghettos. This explosively criminal condition has existed for so long it needs no fuse; it fuses itself."

Few of the reporters seemed to notice during the interview that Malcolm X had undergone a dramatic transformation in his thinking. He had initially become a public figure as a clergyman of the Nation of Islam, a black religious movement that emerged in the United States during the 1930s. Members of the Nation of Islam follow some teachings of the Prophet Muhammad, the seventh-century founder of

Scan here for an excerpt from Malcolm X's May 21, 1964, press conference:

With his Islamic faith serving as the guiding force behind his life and work, Malcolm X made a soul-searching pilgrimage to the holy city of Mecca in the spring of 1964 to visit the birthplace of the Prophet Muhammad, the religion's founder. The Prophet Muhammad's teachings are contained within the Islamic holy scriptures, written in Arabic.

the religion of Islam. However, the Nation of Islam differs from orthodox Islam in many ways, due to the additional teachings of the Nation's founder, W.D. Fard, and his successor, Elijah Muhammad. They wanted to create a separate black nation within the United States. Like most followers of the Nation of Islam (who are known as Black Muslims), Malcolm had learned to view all whites as "devils" and had indicated his allegiance to the Nation by changing his name from Malcolm Little to Malcolm X. (For many Black Muslims, bold-looking letter Xs are used to replace the surnames given to their ancestors by slave owners.)

Malcolm X, however, had recently separated from the movement and altered his views on America's racial problems. He had converted to a mainstream form

THE SIGNIFICANCE OF X

When he became a full member of the Nation of Islam, Malcolm dropped his "slave name" of Little and adopted the last name of "X." It was an important break with the life he had once led. To Malcolm and other members of the Nation of Islam, "X" represented the name and heritage that slaves lost when they were shipped from Africa to the United States.

As slaves, blacks answered to whatever names their masters wanted to call them; they rarely had a last name. Common first names included Sambo, Prince, and Ben. After the Civil War ended in 1865, freed slaves had to decide what to call themselves. Many took the last name of their former master. There were two reasons for this. First, most former slaves had no idea what their original names were. More important, because slaves were considered property—and were bought and sold at their masters' discretion—families were inevitably torn apart. Husbands were frequently separated from their wives, and children from their parents and siblings. In an effort to reunite with family members after the Civil War, many former slaves placed ads in newspapers. Using the last name of a former master afforded a better chance of success.

During the twentieth century, it began to become more common for black Americans who wanted to reconnect to their cultural roots in Africa to take a name that evoked an African identity, and organizations like the Nation of Islam strongly encouraged converts to abandon their "slave names."

of Islam, unlike the version that the Nation of Islam preached in its mosques. While visiting the Middle East, he saw Muslims of many different races sharing a common bond of friendship. Deeply affected by what he witnessed on his travels, he told the press, "I have become convinced that some whites do want to help cure the rampant racism which is on the path to destroying this country."

Malcolm X left the interview knowing that despite having spoken of the urgent need for an improvement in race relations, the headlines in the morning papers would most likely proclaim: MALCOLM X ADVOCATES ARMED NEGROES! He had already grown accustomed to having inaccurate stories printed about him. So long as he urged blacks to resist racial oppression "by any means necessary," he would continue to carry with him a reputation as the one person who could either start or stop a race riot. "I don't know if I could start one," he said, but "I don't know if I'd want to stop one." It is not that he hoped to see a wave of destructive violence sweep through America, but he believed something must be done to jolt his countrymen into understanding that the black

> In July 1964, the shooting of a black youth by a New York City policeman touched off demonstrations in which marchers carried posters of the culpable officer and chanted, "We want justice!" These protests soon exploded into a massive riot in the black ghettos in Harlem and Brooklyn.

CHAPTER 1: THE CITIES ARE BURNING

ghettos were filled with a terrible sense of desperation.

As feared, riots broke out in New York later in the summer—a single incident was all that was needed to set off a neighborhood already seething with frustration and hatred for an overbearing police force that acted more like an occupying army than an agency of justice. A 15-year-old student in the black district of Harlem was shot and killed by a police officer on July 16, 1964. For the next week, the streets of Harlem and the Bedford-Stuyvesant section of Brooklyn became a battle zone filled with gunfire and flaming buildings. The cities had begun to burn, and the fury felt by blacks in the ghettos would soon cause many more cities to be set ablaze.

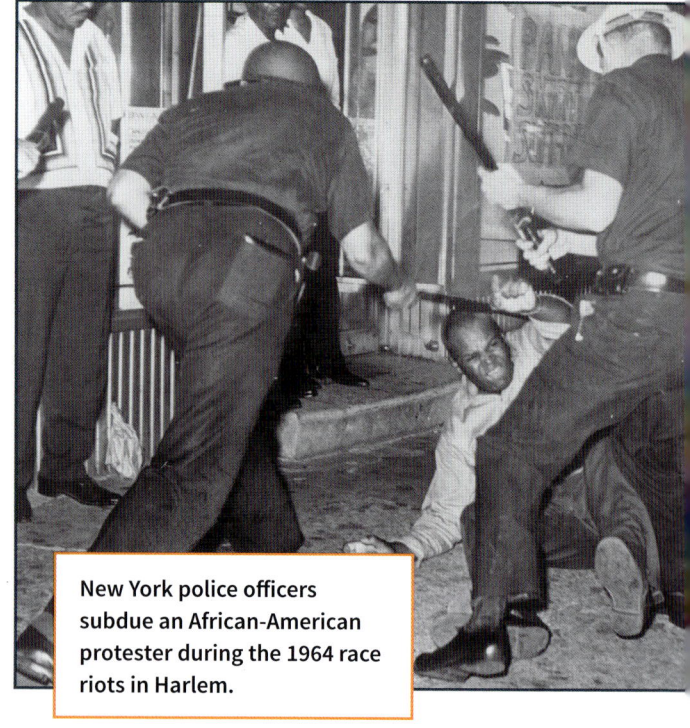

New York police officers subdue an African-American protester during the 1964 race riots in Harlem.

This was Malcolm X's world—a violent world, seething with tension, like a time bomb about to explode. Once the fuse was lit, the changes he had been longing for seemed close at hand.

RESEARCH PROJECT

Using the internet or your school library, do some research to answer the question, "Is violence ever justified?" On one hand, some people argue that the principle of "an eye for an eye" would leave the whole world blind. If people are strong enough, they contend, they can overcome evil with love. Others believe that while violence is wrong, it may also be the lesser of two evils—for example, it is good to overthrow a dictator whose actions cause innocent people to suffer. Present your conclusion in a two-page report, providing examples from your research that support your answer.

TEXT-DEPENDENT QUESTIONS

1. What were the Blood Brothers?
2. What was Malcolm X's ultimate goal?
3. What experience in 1964 helped to change Malcolm X's ideas about race?

From his birth, Malcolm X lived in a world of racism and violence. Malcolm's father was a Baptist minister who was targeted by the Ku Klux Klan (seen here in the early 1920s), and possibly killed by members of a white supremacist group in Michigan.

WORDS TO UNDERSTAND

congregation—a group of people who assemble regularly, often for religious worship.

Jim Crow laws—these were laws passed to enforce segregation based on race. They allowed for separate schools, public transportation, restaurants, and more based on race.

segregation—the separation of people in their daily lives based on race.

white supremacy—a belief that white people are superior to people of all other races, especially the black race, and should therefore dominate society.

16   CIVIL RIGHTS LEADERS: MALCOLM X

CHAPTER 2

A CHALLENGING CHILDHOOD

Malcolm X was born on May 19, 1925, in Omaha, Nebraska. The fourth of Earl and Louise Little's eight children, Malcolm Little (as he was then called) entered a world full of violence and fear. Only a few weeks before his birth, the dreaded night riders of the Ku Klux Klan, the most notorious group dedicated to **white supremacy** in America, paid a visit to his family. The Klan's terrorist attack—part of its campaign to intimidate anyone who was not white and Anglo-Saxon—was the first in a series of grim incidents that devastated Malcolm's family during his early life.

Malcolm's father, Earl, was a strong-willed and outspoken Baptist minister who happened to be preaching in another community on the night when a band of white-robed horsemen appeared at his home. Waving torches and rifles, the Klan members surrounded the house and called for the Reverend Earl Little to step outside. They planned on lynching him in full view of his family.

Malcolm's visibly pregnant mother, Louise, was alone in the house with her three children: Wilfred, Philbert, and Hilda. Although terrified by the ring of fire formed by the horsemen outside her home, she walked out on the porch and told the Klansmen her husband was away on business. Disappointed, they smashed the windows of the house with their rifle butts and warned her that her husband had better leave town.

Earl Little was not the sort of person who bowed before anyone because of intimidation. Born in Reynolds, Georgia, he had grown up in the South in an atmosphere of racial violence. Three of his brothers had been killed by whites.

The attacks were part of the bloody drama staged throughout much of the South after the Civil War. Constitutional amendments had granted citizenship and the right to vote to blacks in 1868 and 1870, but Southern whites were determined to deny them these privileges and other rights of American citizens. The Ku Klux Klan, or KKK, had been formed in 1866 by a group of Confederate Civil War veterans in Pulaski, Tennessee. It soon grew into a large, powerful organization that was dedicated to keeping African Americans from claiming their rights. Across the South,

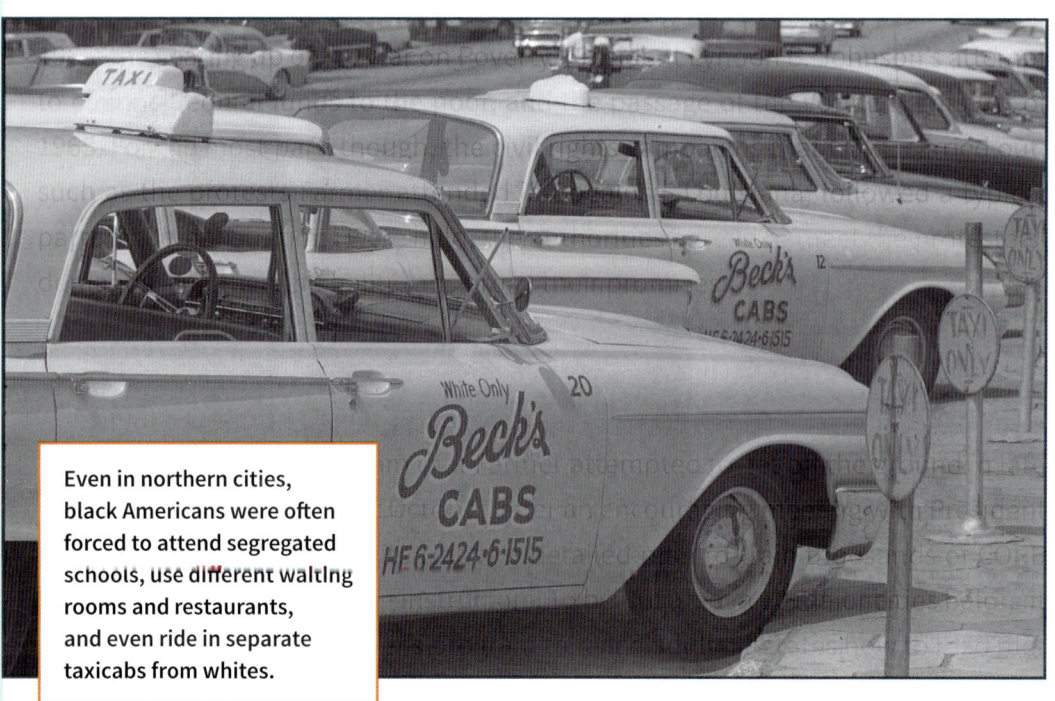

Even in northern cities, black Americans were often forced to attend segregated schools, use different waiting rooms and restaurants, and even ride in separate taxicabs from whites.

To learn more about the KKK in the 1920s, scan here:

members of the Klan and similar organizations terrorized blacks, as well as whites sympathetic to African Americans. Often striking at night, the KKK burned houses and pulled people from their beds to beat or murder them. Victims' bodies were frequently left hanging from trees as a warning that blacks should "stay in their place." To keep from being recognized, Klan members wore white robes and hoods that covered their faces and heads.

In 1871, Congress passed the Force Bill, which gave the federal government broad powers to suppress the KKK's activities. The violence against freed blacks subsided, though it did not end completely.

Whites in the South had other methods to keep blacks as second-class citizens. Through racially discriminatory **Jim Crow laws** established by state legislatures, they prohibited blacks from using the same facilities—including schools, hospitals, theaters, and railroad cars—as whites. Those who protested against the unfair system of racial **segregation** were often beaten. A great many others were lynched. The Klan experienced a resurgence in the mid-1910s, and a burning cross in front of the homes of victims became the new Klan's calling card.

MARCUS GARVEY

Malcolm X's father, Earl Little, was an activist for Marcus Garvey's Universal Negro Improvement Association (UNIA). Young Malcolm attended UNIA meetings with his father and was impressed by the organization's militant stance and Garvey's colorful uniforms.

Marcus Garvey was born in Jamaica on August 17, 1887. He attended school for seven years before becoming a printer and quickly joined the printers' union. At the age of 20, he was elected vice president of the compositors' branch of the printers' union and helped lead a strike before the union dissolved.

In 1911, Garvey moved to England. While studying at Birbeck College, he met blacks from British colonies who were working to achieve their countries' independence. Impressed by their commitment, Garvey returned to Jamaica determined to better the status of his people. He established the UNIA there, and by 1916 had traveled to the United States to organize American branches of his new organization. Its message—urging action against lynching, Jim Crow laws, and racial discrimination—was very popular among blacks. By 1919, the UNIA had more than two million members and 30 branches.

Garvey soon adopted the stance that American whites would never agree to end discrimination and treat blacks as equals. He began to advocate the creation of a separate, independent nation in Africa where all blacks would live. He suggested arming a military unit to seize African territory from any whites who had settled there, and, in a highly controversial move, met with members of the Ku Klux Klan to discuss the planned relocation of all blacks to Africa.

Garvey formed a navigation and trading company and urged his black supporters to invest in it. Financial irregularities plagued the company, however, and Garvey was arrested and charged with fraud. He served half of his five-year prison sentence before being deported to Jamaica.

Garvey attempted to win a seat in Jamaica's colonial legislature but lost the election. He lectured throughout Europe and Canada and eventually moved to England. He died in London in 1940. Ironically, despite his calls for a "Back to Africa" movement, Africa remained one continent that the well-traveled activist never visited.

Jamaican-born Marcus Garvey advocated for black separatism.

CHAPTER 2: A CHALLENGING CHILDHOOD

Malcolm's father took up preaching because it enabled him to speak out for black rights under the protection of the church. After being ordained as a Baptist minister, he moved to Philadelphia, Pennsylvania. There he married and had three children with a woman whom he subsequently divorced. He then married Louise and started a new family.

A restless man who was given to wandering from place to place, Earl Little moved with Louise and his growing family to Omaha, where he started a small farm to supplement the earnings he made as a minister. He also became an activist for Marcus Garvey's Universal Negro Improvement Association (UNIA), a militant organization that urged blacks to stop trying to integrate themselves into white society; the UNIA maintained that they should leave America instead and establish an independent black nation in Africa as part of a "Back to Africa" movement. It was largely because of his position as a spokesman for this black nationalist movement that Malcolm's father was targeted by the Klan.

A MOVE TO MICHIGAN

Shortly after the Klan's attack—and Malcolm's birth—the Littles joined many other black families who left their farms in the South and Midwest and moved to industrial centers in the North, where there seemed to be greater economic opportunities. Malcolm's family stayed briefly in Milwaukee, Wisconsin. Then they settled in Lansing, Michigan, where his father planned to run a store while continuing his preaching.

At first, Lansing seemed to be a place where the family could put down roots. In this Northern town—far from the violent racism he had experienced elsewhere—Earl Little felt he could establish a strong black rights organization. He soon discovered, however, that the ugly specter of racial oppression that had haunted him in the South was also present in the North.

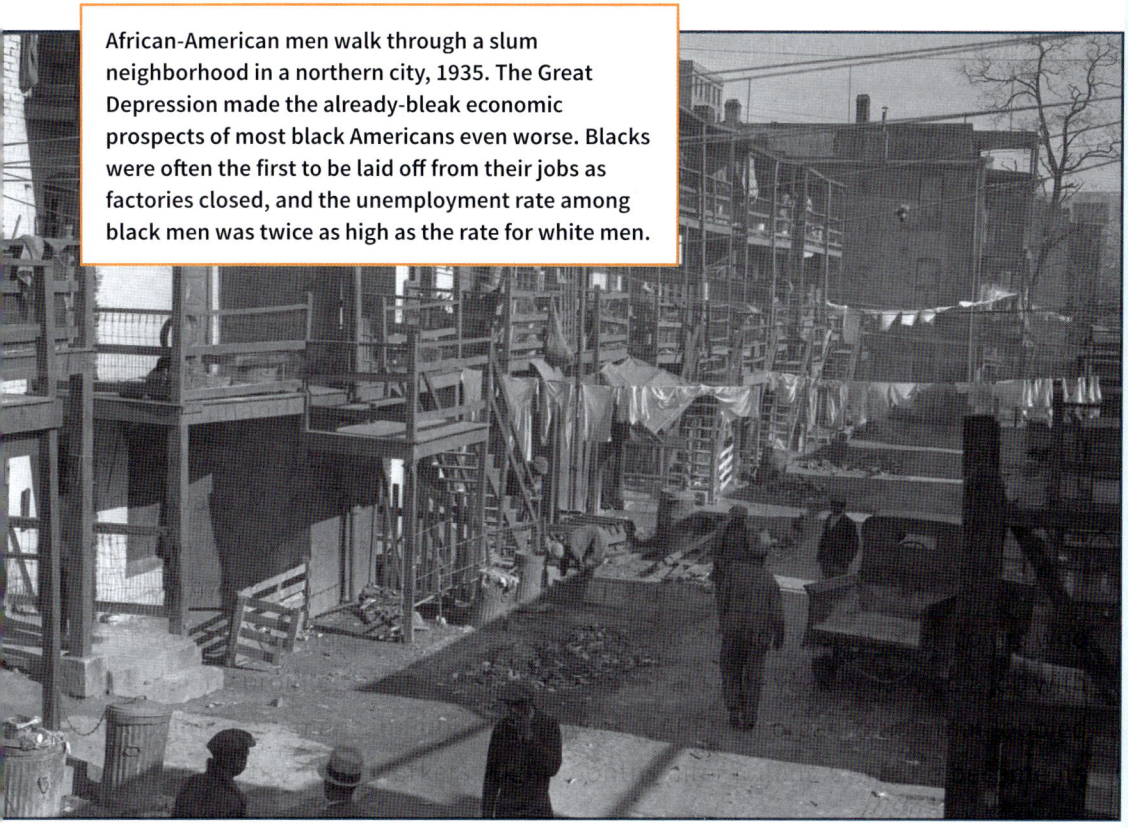

African-American men walk through a slum neighborhood in a northern city, 1935. The Great Depression made the already-bleak economic prospects of most black Americans even worse. Blacks were often the first to be laid off from their jobs as factories closed, and the unemployment rate among black men was twice as high as the rate for white men.

When Malcolm was four years old, night riders again attacked his family. A local group of white supremacists, wearing black robes and calling themselves the Black Legion, had become aware of Earl Little's efforts to organize the black community and had decided to stop him. This time, instead of surrounding his house on horseback, the night riders crept up and set fire to his home.

Malcolm's father ran outside with a pistol and fired at the men after yelling a warning to his family. As flames engulfed their home, Malcolm and his siblings scrambled through the doorway; their mother escaped with the baby, Yvonne, just seconds before the walls caved in. It was a nightmarish scene that became vividly implanted in Malcolm's memory.

CHAPTER 2: A CHALLENGING CHILDHOOD

The Littles failed to receive any assistance from the police, who were more interested in Earl Little's gun than his attackers. In fact, after the Littles settled in a new home in the nearby town of East Lansing, the police raided the house on several occasions in search of the pistol. The gun, hidden in a pillowcase, was never discovered.

Life in East Lansing was just as unpleasant for the Littles as it had been in Lansing. East Lansing had a curfew forbidding blacks to be outdoors after sundown; the ordinance was too much for the Littles to tolerate. They moved to a four-room house built by Malcolm's father on a plot of land a few miles outside of town. Their new home included a garden and a pen for chickens and turkeys.

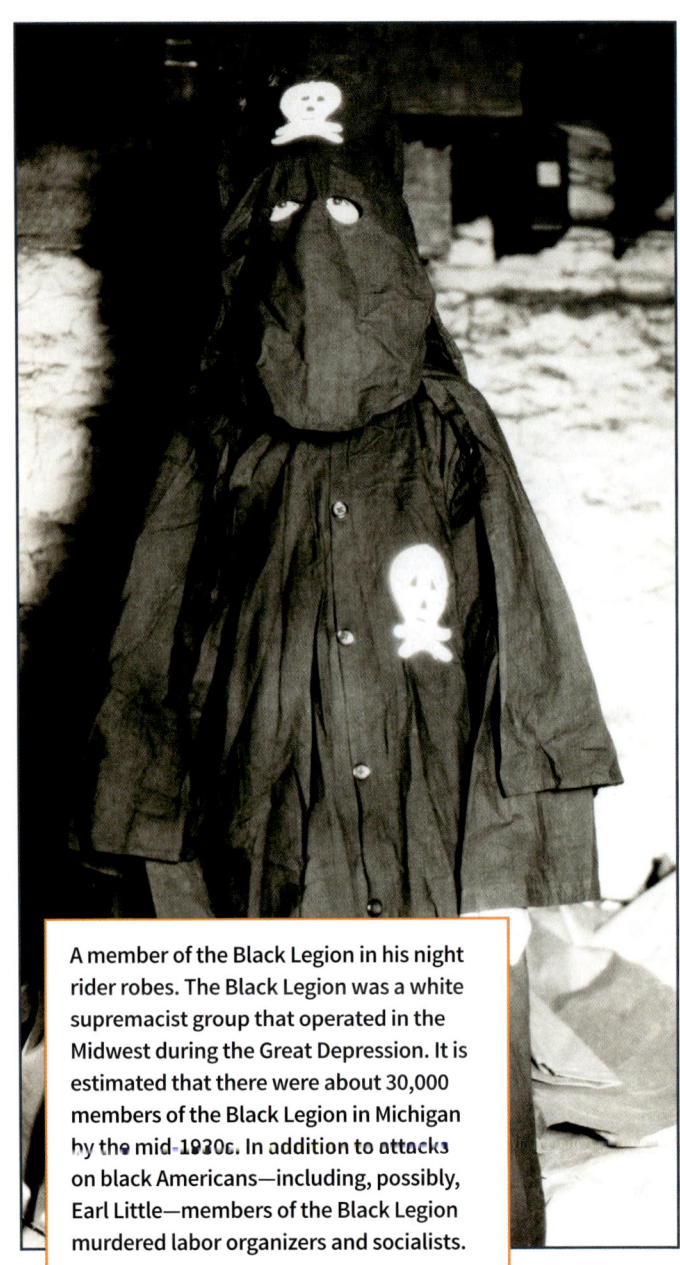

A member of the Black Legion in his night rider robes. The Black Legion was a white supremacist group that operated in the Midwest during the Great Depression. It is estimated that there were about 30,000 members of the Black Legion in Michigan by the mid-1930s. In addition to attacks on black Americans—including, possibly, Earl Little—members of the Black Legion murdered labor organizers and socialists.

The modest farm helped the Littles cope with the ravaging effects of the Great Depression, which occurred after the New York Stock Exchange crashed in the fall of 1929. Industrial centers in the North—including the automobile factories around Lansing—were especially hard hit by the failing economy, and the area's blacks were the hardest hit of all. White workers, victims of soaring unemployment, started to seize the low-paying jobs previously held only by blacks.

Courting the area's dissatisfied blacks, Earl Little continued to hold secret meetings for members of Garvey's Universal Negro Improvement Association. Malcolm, who sometimes accompanied his father to these meetings, was impressed by a picture he saw of Garvey; the founder of the UNIA was garbed in an ornate uniform complete with a plumed hat. The young boy was equally thrilled by an anthem sung at the meetings: "Up, You Mighty Race." The lyrics, which told Garvey's followers, "You can accomplish what you will!," filled Malcolm with confidence that times would improve.

This sense of optimism did not last for long. One day in 1931, after he had engaged in a loud argument with his wife, Earl Little stormed out of the house and was not seen for several hours. He was later found on a section of trolley tracks in downtown East Lansing. One side of his head had been beaten in, and a trolley car had run over him, cutting him almost in half. Astonishingly, he clung to life for more than two hours before he died. His family and friends were sure that members of the Black Legion had attacked him and left him on the tracks to die, although his murderers were never found.

The night riders, it seemed, had finally destroyed Earl Little. Yet the preacher from Georgia left a militant legacy to those who had listened to his calls for black unity. Among them was his six-year-old son Malcolm, who already knew more than any child should know about death and violence.

STRUGGLING FOR SURVIVAL

The death of Earl Little left his family in dire straits. For a year, Louise Little was able to provide for the family after receiving payments from one of two life insurance policies her husband had taken out on himself. The second insurance company refused to make any payments, claiming that Earl Little had committed suicide. Louise Little protested that the ruling was ridiculous, but she never received the money owed her.

Left without its chief provider during the worst years of the depression, Malcolm's family struggled to survive. His oldest brother, Wilfred, dropped out of school and took on any small jobs he could find. Having always been a housewife, Louise Little was unprepared for the burden of supporting eight children by herself (Yvonne, Reginald, Wesley, and Robert were born after Malcolm). She had to leave her children in the care of her oldest daughter, Hilda, while she looked for work. At times, Louise was able to find jobs as a seamstress or maid in the homes of East Lansing's white families, who assumed because of her light skin that she was white. When her prejudiced employers discovered that she was black, she was usually fired on the spot.

The Littles often had no more to eat than a bowl of cornmeal or dandelion greens. Yet they managed to scrape by with some help from friends and neighbors. After Louise Little became a member of the Seventh Day Adventists, one of the few religious groups that ignored America's color line, the family dinner table began to include items contributed by other **congregation** members. Because the Adventists were opposed to eating pork, however, Louise had to refuse some of the donations of sympathetic neighbors. Malcolm and his brother Philbert contributed by hunting for rabbits and bullfrogs, which they sold to white families.

An energetic and restless boy with a light, coppery complexion and dark reddish hair that set him apart from his darker-skinned siblings, Malcolm often fought with his brothers. At the local school, however, where he and the other Little children were the only black students, they banded together to defend themselves against white classmates. From a young age, Malcolm learned to harden himself against the racial slurs that other students used in his presence.

For a short while, it appeared that the Littles might be able to survive as a family: Louise met a man who seemed interested in marrying her. When he stopped visiting her, perhaps overwhelmed by the thought of becoming a stepfather to eight children, she sank into a state of listlessness and took little notice of what was going on around her. She found it impossible to take on steady work, and she was forced to apply to the state welfare department for financial assistance.

The intrusion of state welfare agents into their lives was a demoralizing blow to the family. The welfare agents asked the children why Malcolm's skin color was so much lighter than his brothers' and sisters' and why their mother refused to let them eat pork when they were starving. Such questions confused the children and created tensions and divisions within the family.

In 1940, Malcolm moved to this house in Boston to live with his half-sister, Ella. He was fascinated by the activity and fast-paced nature of the city, and hoped it would provide him with excitement and opportunities.

CHAPTER 2: A CHALLENGING CHILDHOOD

By the time Malcolm was 10, he began to stay away from home, where he was continually reminded of his family's poverty. He spent most evenings at the home of the Gohannases, a black couple who were raising a nephew about Malcolm's age. He also spent time with a group of young men (both black and white) who sometimes met at night to engage in such pranks as pushing over outhouses on nearby farms.

Malcolm soon turned to more criminal acts. He drifted up and down the streets of Lansing during the afternoons, stealing candy, fruit, and other items from stores. He was caught many times, until finally the local court authorities decided that Louise could no longer control Malcolm. They determined to put him in someone else's charge, in part so he would not be a bad influence on his brothers and sisters. Malcolm was relieved when the Gohannases volunteered to take him into their household, for the tensions at his own home had become unbearable.

In 1937, shortly after Malcolm was separated from his family, the state welfare department committed his mother to a mental hospital, where she was to remain for the next 26 years. The Little children became wards of the state, and most of them were sent to live with families in the area. Only Wilfred and Hilda, who were by then old enough to be on their own, were allowed to stay in the Little house.

Malcolm's bitter feelings toward the state authorities, whom he blamed for destroying his family, sometimes boiled over, especially when he was in school. Although he was a very intelligent young man and usually earned good grades, he frequently disrupted the classroom. Finally, he was expelled from school and placed in a juvenile detention center in Mason, Michigan, a town about 20 miles from Lansing, before being sent on to reform school.

The change in Malcolm's surroundings seemed to calm him down a little. Like all but the most violent children at the detention center, he had his own room and ate his meals with the facility's directors, a white couple whose last name was the

Swerlin. Malcolm could be quite charming when he wanted to be, and the Swerlins took an immediate liking to their newest ward and appreciated his eagerness to help with the center's chores.

When the time came for Malcolm to be sent to a reform school, the Swerlins asked him if he wanted to stay with them while he finished his education. He readily agreed to their proposal and was enrolled in Mason's junior high school, whose student body was predominantly white. This time at school, however, his behavior was much improved, and so were his grades: He ranked third in his class academically. He became so popular with the other students that at the end of his first year at Mason, he was elected vice-president of his class.

On the surface, Malcolm seemed to be getting along well with the Swerlins and his classmates. Underneath, though, he was deeply troubled by their attitude toward him and other blacks. The Swerlins used derogatory terms to refer to blacks without realizing the impact of their words on Malcolm. He was popular among the students, he thought, only because they found him strange and exotic, not because they really liked him or cared about his feelings. As he would write later in *The Autobiography of Malcolm X*, "Even though [whites] appeared to open the door, it was still closed." The white world did not want to accept him as an equal.

A NEW LIFE

In the spring of 1939, Malcolm received a letter from his half-sister Ella, a child from his father's first marriage. She had become a successful businesswoman and community leader in Boston, Massachusetts. She was also known to be generous in helping her relatives. Having heard what had befallen her father's second family, she had written to Malcolm and his siblings to find out if she could visit them later in the year to see if she could help them, too.

During her visit with the Littles, Ella discovered that she and Malcolm shared many characteristics, including an enthusiastic approach to life. She invited him to spend the following summer with her in Boston. It was an invitation he was quick to accept.

When Malcolm arrived in Boston, he discovered that Ella lived in the wealthiest part of Roxbury, one of the predominantly black sections of the city. There he was able to experience for the first time in his life what it was like to be a privileged black. He listened to the articulate discussions of Ella's socialite friends, admired the sharply dressed young men and women, and delighted in the city's lively jazz scene. The bands of such top musicians as Duke Ellington and Count Basie came to Boston and played in packed ballrooms on Friday and Saturday nights.

Fourteen-year-old Malcolm was also a little intimidated by Boston: The pace of life was faster than anything he had ever experienced. Yet big-city life fascinated him, and he quickly felt at home there. He regretted having to return to Michigan when the summer came to an end.

Back in Mason, Malcolm could not stop thinking about Boston. Life in a small town seemed much too limited. When one of his favorite teachers advised him to give up his ambition of becoming a lawyer because there was no place in society for black attorneys, Malcolm gave up on his schoolwork and wrote to Ella, asking if she could arrange for him to move in with her. He was elated when he heard she had secured the agreement of the Michigan state welfare department for his change of residence.

In May 1940, soon after his 15th birthday, Malcolm boarded a bus for the lengthy ride to Boston. Yet the trip went by quickly. The excitement and promise of the city's lights kept spinning around in his imagination. A new world was waiting for him, and he was too inexperienced to know the dangers that lay in wait for him in the city.

RESEARCH PROJECT

Using your school library or the internet, do some research to find out why African Americans were deprived of the right to vote in the decades after the Civil War. Write a two-page report with your conclusions, and share it with your class.

TEXT-DEPENDENT QUESTIONS

1. Who were Malcolm Little's parents?
2. What was the Ku Klux Klan?
3. Why did the Little family move to Michigan?
4. Why did Malcolm Little begin staying away from home when he was ten?
5. What relative invited Malcolm to spend the summer with her in Boston?

For Malcolm Little, the opportunity to hear live jazz in Boston's dance halls was one of the many attractions of living in the city.

WORDS TO UNDERSTAND

boycott—to refuse to buy something or to take part in an activity as a way of protesting certain practices or draw attention to undesirable behaviors.

quell—to put an end to a disorder, often through the use of force.

tenement—a run-down, overcrowded apartment building.

CHAPTER 3

INTO THE UNDERWORLD

Malcolm arrived at Ella's house in the spring of 1940 a mixture of confidence and confusion: Although he looked and acted much older than his 15 years, he was still a tall and skinny teenager whose wrists and ankles jutted out of his light green suit. He immediately made it clear to Ella that he wanted to work rather than go to school. In that case, she told him, he should explore Boston before he found a job; he might never again have a chance to enjoy the city. Except for Ella, though, he had no one to show him around his new hometown.

Malcolm soon found his guide. One day, when he was hanging around a Roxbury pool hall, he met a young man named Shorty who had come to Boston many years before from Lansing, Michigan. Shorty took Malcolm under his wing and helped him find his first job: working as a shoe shiner at the Roseland State Ballroom, one of city's most popular music and dance halls.

Ella was not happy when she heard about Malcolm's new job. As a member of Boston's black elite, she wanted him to find work that was a bit more prestigious. Yet Malcolm had become disenchanted with black high society and believed that many of its members were either snobs, who put on airs, or hypocrites, who would say they were "in banking" when they were only janitors at a bank. Worst of all in his eyes, they were trying to imitate white society.

Malcolm was far more attracted to Roxbury's sporting life than to its black upper class. At his job at Roseland, he was not only among people with whom he felt more comfortable, but he also got to listen to some of the best jazz bands in the country. Like the other black employees in the dance hall, he held a somewhat privileged position, for only white customers were admitted to most shows; the Roseland management opened the hall to blacks just once or twice a month. In 1940, racial segregation was still being practiced in America, even in supposedly liberal Northern cities such as Boston.

Malcolm made money at Roseland by blacking shoes and also earned tips by bringing towels to rest room patrons. He quickly learned he could earn a larger tip than usual by loudly snapping the shoeshine cloth after finishing a job. He learned, too, that white customers liked to have blacks, such as Malcolm, defer to them, and they would pay him better if he bowed his head and acted submissive.

Yet Malcolm did not always act so innocently at Roseland. He supplemented his earnings by selling marijuana to some of the customers and by letting them know how to get in touch with the local prostitutes. He had few reservations about dealing in these kinds of illegal activities. They seemed acceptable ways of making a living because, he believed, he had little chance at being offered a reputable and well-paying job.

As he became more involved in Roxbury's world of drugs, drinking, and gambling, Malcolm developed an appetite for these vices as well. The more money he had to spend, the more he indulged. He also became hooked on dancing, especially a wild dance called the Lindy Hop. Named after Charles Lindbergh, the first aviator to pilot a plane across the Atlantic Ocean, the dance imitated an airplane taking off and landing as female dancers were thrown into the air and caught by their partners.

To go with his new lifestyle, Malcolm invested in a new wardrobe. He replaced his ill-fitting green suit with a sky-blue zoot suit, which featured baggy pants and a long, tight-waisted coat, and he added to it a blue felt hat and a gold pocketwatch

Scan here for a short video on conk hairstyles:

chain that hung to his knees. He completed his new look by having his red hair "conked," or straightened: Conks were popular among young blacks in the ghetto, even though the lye used to straighten their hair also burned their scalp.

Later in his life, Malcolm viewed his conk hairstyle as "my first really big step toward self-degradation"—an act that symbolized his rejection of his black features and indicated his desire to appear more white. At the time, he looked on himself as being what was then known in the ghettos as a "hip cat." He was set on using his good looks and smart appearance to get what he wanted: money, women, and excitement.

Malcolm eventually quit his shoeshine job at Roseland because it interfered with his desire to be out on Roxbury's streets at night. He worked for a while as a soda fountain clerk at a drugstore near Ella's house. There, much to his half sister's delight, he met a proper young woman named Laura, whom he began taking to dances.

Malcolm and Laura had not been dating for very long, however, before he met a white woman named Sophia at a Roseland dance contest. Fascinated by the cool, sophisticated Sophia, Malcolm ended his relationship with Laura and began spending his nights hopping from barroom to barroom with Sophia. He was deaf to Ella's protests about his activities because his white girlfriend represented for him a glamorous new life. He was intoxicated with the world and grew impatient to see as much of it as he could. High on his list of places to visit was Harlem, the New York City district that boasted the largest black population in the country.

Zoot suits, "conked" hair, and flashy shoes were all part of the "hip cat" image that Malcolm Little and other style-conscious young black men tried to cultivate in the early 1940s.

HARLEM BLUES

In December 1941, after the United States entered World War II, Malcolm finally found the opportunity to go to Harlem. Not only was the economy picking up, but job openings throughout the country were becoming plentiful because so many men were enlisting in the army. Malcolm, by lying about his age, was able to get a job selling sandwiches on the Yankee Clipper passenger train, which made daily runs between Boston and New York.

The 16-year-old hip cat was as awed by New York as he had been amazed by Boston a year and a half earlier. He was especially overwhelmed by Harlem, which in the early 1900s had become the leading center of black American culture and politics. During his first trip there, which included a visit to a popular nightclub called Small's Paradise, he gawked at the sheer number of people bustling around him, almost all of whom were black. It was as if Harlem were a whole city of black people, a world where racial prejudice was hidden away in the background. "I was mesmerized," he said later. "This world was where I belonged. On that night I had started on my way to becoming a Harlemite."

Malcolm moved out of Ella's house after he began working on the Yankee Clipper and rented a room in a Harlem boardinghouse. He attended the shows of such musical performers as Dizzy Gillespie and Billie Holiday on his days off from work. In Harlem's entertainment district, he befriended musicians who played at such noted dance halls as the Apollo Theater and the Savoy Ballroom.

No longer under Ella's watchful eye, Malcolm behaved more wildly in New York than he had in Boston. He dyed his hair bright red, stayed high on marijuana, and acted outrageously on the Yankee Clipper, racing up and down the train in the belief that his customers would give him larger tips if he entertained them. Yet he often crossed the line between entertainment and insult. Passengers filed complaints against him, and although he was warned to stop using profane language, he continued to act out of control. Finally, he was fired. At age 17, he was, he would later admit, "an uncouth, wild young Negro. I was really a clown, but my ignorance made me think I was sharp."

Malcolm found a job waiting tables in his favorite hangout, Small's Paradise, after he was fired by the railroad. While working there, he listened with fascination to the stories of the notorious Harlem underworld figures who gathered at the club. These men, who included the old pickpocket Fewclothes, the gambling racketeer West Indian Archie, and a group of garment-district mobsters known as the Forty

THE ALLURE OF HARLEM

Malcolm Little's main objective when he first arrived in Harlem was to have a good time. He was dazzled by the lights, the clubs, and the prosperous black people who enjoyed Harlem's nightlife.

Located in New York City's borough of Manhattan, Harlem was first settled by the Dutch in the 1600s. Small groups of black people were living in Harlem as early as 1880, primarily in rundown buildings called **tenements**. More blacks arrived after the turn of the century. Many came from the South. By the end of World War I in 1918, Harlem was an overwhelmingly black neighborhood.

During the 1920s, Harlem became arguably the most important center of black culture in the United States. The "Harlem Renaissance" is the name given to the explosion of poetry, literature, music, sculpture, photography, and art by black Americans during this period. Entertainment was also a vital part of day-to-day life. In addition to the famous Apollo Theater and Savoy Ballroom, there were dozens of cafés, taverns, supper clubs, and dance halls throughout Harlem.

By the 1940s, Harlem's clubs and theaters had also become popular among whites. There, fans of jazz music could see performers like Duke Ellington, Count Basie, Ella Fitzgerald, and Dinah Washington.

Sixteen-year-old Malcolm Little was briefly employed as a sandwich seller on a railroad lounge car. He was dismissed from the job because he had used drugs and alcohol and was rude to passengers.

Thieves, were veterans of the streets. They knew all the tricks of hustling: how to make damaged merchandise seem like valuable goods, where to hide drugs so the police could not find them, how to persuade gambling clients to pay their debts. They were quite willing to share their secrets with Malcolm. In fact, one of the Forty Thieves gave Malcolm an expensive new suit, a sign of acceptance into their ranks.

Malcolm's entry into the Harlem underworld was not accompanied by any fears that he was making a wrong decision. He did not believe he could make a living at a more respectable occupation. He also realized that hustling was a desperate gamble and enriched few who tried it. "Everybody in Harlem needed some kind of hustle to survive," he said, "and needed to stay high in some way to forget what they had to do to survive."

For the most part, Malcolm was careful not to risk his job at Small's by hustling at the club. One day, however, he told a lonely looking soldier where he could find a prostitute. The "soldier" was actually a police informant, and Malcolm was fired from the club.

Although Malcolm regretted losing his position, he decided not to take another legitimate job. He cared little about moral questions or the consequences of his actions. He saw himself as a smart, cynical loner. The key to success in life, he felt,

White sailors gamble on a dice game in New York City. During World War II, New York was a major port of call for U.S. servicemen. Malcolm Little, in his role as a hustler, encountered many of the soldiers who traveled to Harlem in search of a little nightlife before leaving for duty overseas.

was to use other people more than they used him. "A man," he believed, "should do anything that he was slick enough, or bad and bold enough, to do."

Malcolm wanted to become a full-time hustler, and for advice on how to succeed in hustling he turned to Sammy the Pimp, a friend who lived in the same boardinghouse. After Sammy advised him to start dealing drugs on the street, Malcolm plied his new trade energetically, selling marijuana to his musician friends. Older hustlers noted his successful business and decided to give him a nickname that would distinguish him as an underworld operator. Because he had grown up in Michigan and had a dyed conk, they soon began calling him Detroit Red.

Malcolm's drug dealing brought him some money at the beginning, until the police took notice of his activities. They began to follow him on the streets, sometimes stopping him and frisking him. He was never caught carrying any illegal drugs, having learned ways to quickly conceal marijuana packets whenever he saw a policeman approach.

One evening, however, Malcolm came home and discovered his apartment had been searched while he was out. He never kept his drugs at home, but he believed that the police had planted a concealed packet somewhere. Afraid they would soon raid his apartment, he decided to leave. For the next year, he was constantly on the move from one rooming house to the next, always fearful of a knock on the door.

LIFE OF CRIME

When Malcolm turned 18 in May 1943, he became eligible to be drafted into the army. Ordered to appear before his local draft board, he arrived at the induction center in his most outrageous zoot suit, determined to be disqualified from military service. While being examined by an army psychiatrist, he kept up a rapid, nonsensical banter that he stopped only so he could leap out of his chair and look under closet doors for intruders. Then he claimed he was planning to organize a bloody revolt of black soldiers against whites at army bases in the South. The shocked psychiatrist dropped his pencil. Malcolm was subsequently declared psychologically unfit for the army.

Malcolm's exaggerated behavior at the army induction center was only a show, but his real emotional condition was actually becoming frayed. His constant movement to new living quarters and his anxiety about being arrested had begun to make him feel like a hunted animal. His regular market among Harlem musicians had been closed off because of police surveillance, and he was forced to sell drugs to addicts in the most depressed parts of Harlem. His new customers were a desperate and dangerous group, and Malcolm said that in going into the worst ghetto areas, "You enter a world of animals and vultures. It becomes truly the survival of only the fittest."

Street scene in Harlem, 1943. In August of that year, a fight between a white policeman and a black soldier sparked a riot that left six people dead and more than 400 wounded. About 16,000 police and civilian volunteers were rushed in to restore order, but not before Harlem's business district was devastated by the rioters.

Detroit Red thrashed around while trying to find a more lucrative hustle, but he was slowly being dragged down by his own game. Hounded so closely by the police that he was shut out from selling drugs in Harlem, he turned in desperation to armed robbery. After buying some guns, he traveled to towns outside New York and held up people on the streets. He soon found he had to be under the influence of cocaine or some other narcotic to be able to perform a robbery, and his heavy use of drugs hastened his downward slide.

By 1943, Malcolm was living in constant fear not only of the police but also of Harlem's underworld kingpins. On at least one occasion, he was roughed up by mobsters who suspected him of robbing one of their businesses. He lived with an arsenal of pistols, and tucking his compact .25 automatic "streetwear" into his waistband before leaving his apartment became as natural a habit as tying his shoelaces in the morning. "Full-time hustlers never can relax to appraise what they are doing and where they are bound," he later said. "If he ever relaxes, if he ever slows down, the other hungry restless foxes, ferrets, wolves, and vultures out there with him won't hesitate to make him their prey."

Economic conditions in Harlem, which were severe during the Great Depression, continued to deteriorate during World War II, and hustlers were driven into trying ever more dangerous ways to make money. While attempting to break into a heavily protected building, Malcolm and his friend Sammy were surprised by security guards and were fired upon. Both men escaped, but Sammy was slightly wounded.

After the aborted robbery, the security guards' description of Malcolm was posted on "Wanted" notices around Harlem. He decided to give up robbery and find a new occupation, but the only activities on which he seemed to be able to focus his attention were dreaming up new hustles, gambling, and taking narcotics.

CURRENT OF DISCONTENT

As Malcolm was facing an increasingly bleak future, racial tensions in Harlem were growing. Harlemites, like other black Americans, were incensed that blacks who enlisted in the army were forced to serve in segregated units and were given almost no opportunity to become officers. During a period when Americans were being asked to make sacrifices to help the war effort against Germany and Japan, many blacks were being lynched in the South, harassed in Northern ghettos, and excluded from well-paying jobs in the defense industry.

In Harlem, a rising young politician and preacher named Adam Clayton Powell, Jr., organized **boycotts** against utility companies and white-owned local businesses that practiced racial discrimination. Only limited steps were taken to correct the grievances, however, and an angry current of discontent continued to run through Harlem. Finally, in August 1943, the district erupted after a black soldier was shot by a white policeman in a Harlem hotel. Black mobs roamed the district's streets, smashing the windows of the area's mainly white-owned businesses and looting the stores.

ADAM CLAYTON POWELL, JR.

While Malcolm X was dealing drugs and committing armed robbery, another young black man in Harlem was organizing boycotts against utility companies and other white-owned businesses that practiced racial discrimination. This determined politician and preacher was Adam Clayton Powell, Jr.

Powell was born on November 29, 1908, in New Haven, Connecticut. As a young boy, he moved with his family to New York City, where his father began developing the Abyssinian Baptist Church. He graduated from Colgate University and then received his Master of Arts in religious education from Columbia University. When the Depression ravaged Harlem and the rest of the United States, Powell worked at his father's church, but his focus quickly shifted to the civil rights movement.

Determined to correct the discrimination and poverty crippling the black community, Powell organized rent strikes and boycotts of

Thousands of police were called in to **quell** the riot with a show of force, but blacks fought back, sometimes with rifles and pistols. Before the violence ended, 5 people were dead, more than 400 were injured, and Harlem's business district lay in ruins. Along with many other Harlemites, Malcolm saw the 1943 riot as a gesture of black defiance not only against the white politicians and businessmen who controlled New York City but against a police force regularly accused of assaults on blacks.

Although there were several reasons for the unrest, the riot had a single effect on Harlem: The community was devastated. Whites stopped coming to restaurants, stores, bus lines, telephone companies, and even Harlem Hospital, urging them to hire and promote black employees. From 1936 to 1944, he published *The Peoples Voice,* a newspaper that publicized his efforts to correct injustice and discrimination. In 1945, he was elected to Congress, where he quickly ensured that the informal regulations reserving capitol facilities for white congressional members only were changed.

Throughout his congressional career, Powell clashed with segregationists and worked to ensure that nearly every piece of legislation carried an antidiscrimination rider. His committee work included important measures to approve minimum wage increases, education and training for the deaf, and federal support for student loans and school lunches.

Accused of slander, Powell was investigated by the Judiciary Committee and stripped of his committee chairmanship in 1967. Two years later, a ruling in his favor restored his seat in Congress. He unsuccessfully sought reelection in 1970 before retiring. He died in 1972.

the area, and its once glittering theater district went out of business. The black community became poorer and more isolated than it had ever been before, and unemployment soared.

Malcolm survived by becoming a numbers runner, one of the people who collect tickets for the illegal lottery game controlled by mobsters. Two close scrapes almost cost him his life. First, a mob family suspected him of having robbed one of its dice games, and it sent two gunmen to kill him. Malcolm was inside a phone booth when the mob's executioners found him, and they told him to step outside so that they "could hold court." The verdict had already been given, but fortunately for the accused a policeman suddenly appeared and he was able to walk away.

Malcolm was still in shock from this incident when one of his underworld friends, West Indian Archie, accused him of cheating on a bet. He was told to return the money he had won or suffer the consequences. Only a small amount of money was involved, but each man was determined to protect his reputation. "A hustler could never afford to have it demonstrated that he could be bluffed, that he could be frightened by a threat, that he lacked nerve," Malcolm later said of this incident. The two men finally had a showdown in a Harlem bar, but friends stopped them before it turned into a shoot-out.

Malcolm was walking down a Harlem street two days later when a car pulled up beside him. Instinctively, he pulled out his gun, but stopped and breathed a sigh of relief when he realized that the driver was Shorty, his friend from Boston. He had heard about Malcolm's troubles and had driven to New York to help him out. Six hours later, the two were back in Roxbury.

Malcolm's escape to Boston may have freed him from immediate danger, but it did not rescue him from his destructive habits. He quickly became involved in Roxbury's gambling and numbers operations and also organized a burglary ring with Shorty. His former girlfriend Sophia and her sister scouted out potential targets for his thefts by acting as door-to-door saleswomen.

For a while, Malcolm made a good living by selling stolen goods to pawn shops. His theft ring was finally uncovered when he took a stolen watch to be repaired. The police, on the lookout for the watch, arrested him when he retrieved it at the shop, and he received a ten-year prison sentence for burglary. His hustler's luck had finally run out.

Malcolm had survived several brushes with death, and his wild life had given him a bitter knowledge of the worst of human behavior. Yet when he entered Boston's Charlestown State Prison in February 1946, he was only 20 years old.

RESEARCH PROJECT

Using the internet or your school library, find out about racism in the Northern states during the nineteenth and twentieth centuries. Make a list of ways that black Americans were treated differently in the North from whites, and share it with your class.

TEXT-DEPENDENT QUESTIONS

1. What was Malcolm Little's first job?
2. How did Malcolm supplement his income at Roseland?
3. Why did Malcolm move to Harlem in 1941?
4. What decision did Malcolm make after losing his job at Small's Paradise?
5. What friend brought Malcolm Little back to Boston when he was in trouble?

Malcolm Little spent the first two years of his prison term at Charlestown State Prison in Massachusetts. This primitive, dungeonlike structure was built in Boston in the early 1800s.

WORDS TO UNDERSTAND

eloquence—used to describe language that is fluent and persuasive.
isolation—to be set apart from other people.
solitary confinement—the isolation of a prisoner in a cell separate from the other prisoners, often as punishment.

CHAPTER 4

PRISON EPIPHANY

Malcolm endured a harrowing first few months at Charlestown State Prison. In prison slang, he was a fish (a new inmate), and he did not take well to being in the tank. He was placed in a tiny cell that had a covered bucket for a toilet. He was forced to follow the prison's dreary, inflexible daily routine while suffering withdrawal from the drugs he had been taking. His prisoner number was constantly drilled into him because the authorities never referred to a prisoner by his name.

The metal bars that surrounded Malcolm made him feel like a caged animal. He soon became sullen and defiant, throwing loud temper tantrums and cursing at both the prison psychologist and the chaplain. Eventually, when the guards called out his prison number at roll call in the morning, he refused to answer.

Malcolm was often placed in **solitary confinement** as the prison authorities tried to squash his rebelliousness. Yet the punishment did little to deter his violent behavior, partly because he liked the **isolation**. He would pace his cell furiously, lashing out at everyone and everything until he wore himself out. After resting for a while, he would get up and resume his attacks.

Malcolm took such perverse pride in his violent behavior and his status as an outcast that his fellow inmates gave him the nickname of Satan. He refused to conform to any aspect of prison life. The only thing that seemed to temporarily calm him were the mildly intoxicating spices that prisoners abused as substitutes for hard drugs.

Malcolm felt little beyond an intense hatred of himself and the world. His relatives tried to help him adjust. Ella sometimes met him in the prison's visiting room and his brothers and sisters wrote to him, but during his first two years in jail, he stubbornly resisted all their efforts to reach out to him.

It was a meeting with an older prisoner named Bimbi that would help Malcolm take a first step toward changing his life. A professional burglar and veteran of many prisons, Bimbi had used his time in jail to broaden his mind with the study of such subjects as grammar, history, and philosophy. He was held in great esteem by Charlestown's prisoners, especially because of the **eloquence** with which he defended his opinions.

Malcolm and Bimbi worked together in the prison workshop where license plates were stamped out. One day, when the prisoners had a short break from work, Malcolm made a blistering attack on religion. Bimbi demolished Malcolm's argument without raising his voice or cursing—Malcolm's usual tactics when debating an issue. Bimbi's words did not change Malcolm's views about religion, but it did show him how an intelligent and masterful speaker could take command of an audience.

The young inmate also discovered that he had impressed Bimbi as well. According to the older man, Malcolm had a fine mind, which he could improve by studying in the prison library and taking correspondence courses. Coming from a man whom Malcolm greatly respected, the advice struck home. He decided to enroll in a correspondence course in English grammar.

A WAY OUT OF PRISON

Because Malcolm had dropped out of school in the eighth grade, he had much catching up to do. His natural intelligence and curiosity helped him overcome many

> Malcolm's decision to attend classes at the prison school proved to be a major turning point in his life. "The streets," he said, "had erased everything I'd ever learned in school."

shortcomings, and he soon expanded his studies to include Latin and linguistics. Although his vocabulary and handwriting remained fairly crude, his ability to express his ideas improved bit by bit.

While Malcolm furthered his education, he also began to think about the twists and turns that had led him to a cell in Charlestown. He soon came to realize that broad political and social observations could be drawn from his experiences as a black youth struggling to find a place in American society. Slowly, he transformed himself from a self-centered hustler into a socially conscious black militant.

In 1948, a few months after Malcolm was transferred to a prison in Concord, Massachusetts, Ella persuaded state prison officials to move him to a more modern facility in nearby Norfolk, Massachusetts. The new prison operated under more

NORFOLK PRISON COLONY

Malcolm described the Norfolk State Prison Colony, which he entered in 1948, as too good to be true. Built during the 1930s, it was an experimental jail. The emphasis was not on punishing the prisoners, but on rehabilitating them so that they could leave as productive members of society. Rather than living in cells, prisoners lived in dormitories. Each man had his own room. There were shower rooms, which the prisoners could use as often as they liked, as well as a ball field for those who wanted to exercise, and garden plots for those who liked growing their own food.

At Norfolk, the emphasis was on prisoner education. There were evening courses, in academic subjects as well as in subjects that would train the inmates for future jobs.

One of the most notable features at Norfolk was its library. Its large collection was donated to Massachusetts by Lewis Parkhurst, a state senator. Parkhurst had spent a big part of his career working for prison reform. Many of the books Malcolm read at Norfolk were a testament to Parkhurst's interest in religion and history.

relaxed rules and had a large library, flush toilets, and regular rooms instead of barred cells for each inmate. Malcolm took advantage of the prison's educational program, which featured lectures and debates led by instructors from local colleges, and steadily improved his speaking skills.

During his stay at the Norfolk Prison, Malcolm also developed an interest in religion. His brothers Reginald and Philbert and his sister Hilda had been writing to him for some time about the black religious group known as the Nation of Islam, which they had joined. Malcolm had always responded with crude, sarcastic insults when they told him that they had mentioned his name in prayer meetings. Slowly, though, he became intrigued. He knew he needed something other than rage to give meaning to his life, and he was interested in Reginald's promise that becoming a Black Muslim would ultimately be his ticket to freedom.

In late 1948, Reginald decided to try to lure Malcolm into the fold. He ended a letter to Malcolm with a mysterious proposition. "Don't eat any more pork, and don't smoke any more cigarettes," Reginald told his older brother. "I'll show you how to get out of prison."

Reginald's strange advice had an effect on Malcolm, although not the one Reginald intended. By neither eating pork nor smoking cigarettes (which are observances of the Islamic faith), he might be able to fool the authorities into thinking he had reformed. Perhaps they would then parole him from prison. After all, he had deceived an army psychiatrist once. Why not a prison psychiatrist?

Malcolm abstained from pork and cigarettes while he waited for a visit from Reginald, who was then to reveal the entire scheme. In prison, where the smallest changes in routine are the subject of endless gossip, Malcolm's action set off a chorus of whispers. "Satan doesn't eat pork!" the inmates told one another.

When Reginald finally paid a visit at Norfolk, Malcolm discovered that his brother did not have a magic dietary formula to help him get out of prison. All he had to offer was the Nation of Islam. In response to Malcolm's question about how abstinence from pork and cigarettes could free someone, Reginald offered another question: "If a man knew every imaginable thing that there is to know, who would he be?"

"Well, he would have to be some kind of a god," Malcolm answered.

Reginald replied that there was a man who knew everything. His name was Allah.

Puzzled, Malcolm listened as Reginald described how Allah had a full circle—360 degrees—of knowledge, whereas Allah's enemy, the devil, had only 33 degrees.

Most of Reginald's explanation of the Nation of Islam's teachings was baffling to Malcolm, but two phrases stuck in his mind: "The white man is the devil," and "The black man is brainwashed."

After Reginald left, Malcolm began to think deeply about his own experiences with whites. He and his family had been terrorized by the Ku Klux Klan and split up by white social workers; he had been exploited by white employers, harassed by white policemen, and jailed by white judges. Everywhere he had gone in the ghettos, he had seen poor blacks abandoned by white society.

Again, Malcolm spun through his head the two statements that were the opposite sides of the same coin in the Nation of Islam's theology: The white race was corrupt and was the source of all evil; the members of the black race were Allah's chosen people and were destined to destroy the white devils. To Malcolm, the statements seemed to offer a sound explanation for all the injustice in the world. Moreover, he took great comfort in the prediction that a terrifying doom awaited all whites. He found himself wanting to learn more about the Nation of Islam.

During the next few weeks, Reginald, Hilda, and Philbert wrote to Malcolm almost daily, discussing the philosophy of the Black Muslims and urging him to place himself in the hands of Allah and his supreme prophet, Elijah Muhammad, who headed the Nation of Islam. The more Malcolm learned about Islam, the more focused he felt. Hearing about the supremacy of the black race sparked a sense of inner pride that he had rarely felt since the time when he had attended meetings of the Universal Negro Improvement Association with his father.

Scan here to learn more about the Nation of Islam in prisons:

For years, Malcolm had been drifting through life without any direction. Now, if he wanted to join the Nation of Islam, he would have to accept its theology and submit completely to the authority of Elijah Muhammad. As Malcolm learned more about Elijah Muhammad and the teachings of the Nation of Islam, he saw many parallels with his father's life, and these associations made it easier for him to consider converting to Islam.

THE LIFE OF A PROPHET

Originally named Elijah Poole, Elijah Muhammad was born in 1897 in a rural Georgia community, about 70 miles from where Earl Little was born, and grew up with a strong belief in racial pride and black solidarity. Like Malcolm's father, he, too, moved north in search of better work opportunities and freedom from racial oppression. With his large family, he settled in Detroit.

In 1931, Poole met a small, brown-skinned man named W. D. Fard, who sold silk products door-to-door in Detroit's black ghetto. Fard claimed to be from Arabia and styled himself as a prophet who had come to the United States to help blacks discover their dual African and Islamic heritage. According to Fard, black Americans were descended from the first humans, the "original race," whose descendants could be found in their purest form among Muslims in the Middle East, Africa, and Asia. Fard told black Americans they were Islam's "lost sheep," and he said he and his Nation of Islam faith could help them find their true religion and overcome their white oppressors.

Fard's teachings varied markedly from those of traditional Islam, which teaches brotherhood between people of all races. His religion had many beliefs in common with Marcus Garvey's black nationalist movement and Noble Drew Ali's early twentieth-century Islamic group, the short-lived Moorish Temple of America. Ali, who amassed a wide following by claiming that blacks were superior to whites and the white race was doomed, mysteriously disappeared sometime in the late 1920s. Fard's movement attracted some of the same people who had been drawn to Garvey and Ali.

One of Fard's first converts was Elijah Poole, who changed his name to Elijah Muhammad in accordance with Fard's command that his followers give up their Christian surnames and take Islamic names. Fard told blacks that their Christian surnames were false names because they were probably the names of slave owners who had robbed blacks of their true African names. Some converts used an *X* or combination of *X*s and other letters to symbolize that their true names had been lost and they had become *ex*-slaves.

Fard and Muhammad roused growing support for the Nation of Islam during the early 1930s and established Islamic temples (known as mosques) in converted stores in a number of Midwestern cities. The group's message of black superiority and resistance to white domination appealed especially to the poor blacks of the urban ghettos. Fard's religious doctrines offered these people hope that their hardships would soon end.

> Elijah Muhammad became the leader of the Nation of Islam in 1934. His followers viewed him as the supreme prophet of the militant religion that preached that whites were corrupt and blacks were God's chosen people.

The scriptures that Fard preached were based on Islamic teachings, but they included a strong emphasis on racial doctrines. He taught there was no heaven or hell after death; instead, heaven and hell existed here on earth. Black Americans, according to Fard, had been living in hell for nearly 400 years. This period of slavery and damnation was coming to an end, however, because of the return of the savior for black Americans. In Islamic tradition, this savior is called the Madhi and is considered to be both a person and God. The Madhi, Fard taught, was none other than himself.

The Nation of Islam's beliefs about the beginnings of mankind differed sharply from those of any other religious group. According to Fard, the world was ruled in early times by members of a black race who were known as the original men. These people established a highly advanced civilization, and their scientists populated the earth with animals, created mountains and seas, blasted the moon into the sky from the Pacific Ocean region, and even communicated with a race of nine-foot-tall giants on Mars. The original men lived in peace with each other and worshiped Allah from their holy city of Mecca.

Fard taught that evil had entered the world because a mad scientist named Yacub had let his pride in his scientific knowledge tempt him into breaking the laws of Islam. Exiled from Mecca, the vengeful Yacub had used his knowledge of genetics to create a devil race of vicious, immoral white people. Once loosed upon the world, the lying and scheming white devils caused great trouble for the original people.

Eventually, the whites were herded together and sent to live in caves in the cold wasteland of Europe. Allah sent the black prophets Moses and Jesus to teach the white devils about Islam with the hope of civilizing them. According to Fard, the whites corrupted the prophets' teachings and created the religions of Judaism and Christianity.

Fard maintained that in accordance with an ancient prophecy, the white devils had finally gained control of the world. Once in power, no evil was beyond them. They had enslaved millions of blacks in Africa and transported them to the Americas, where the black captives were stripped of their language, culture, and history and were brainwashed into hating themselves. They were taught that whites were superior in all ways and that God and Jesus were white.

The corrupt reign of the white man was about to end, Fard said. He, the Madhi, had appeared, and he was going to lead the black race back to the original state of grace it had known before the advent of the white man. The time of redemption was at hand.

The aim of the Nation of Islam was to restore to blacks their cultural heritage and racial identity. The Nation claimed that centuries of slavery and oppression, which included slave auctions like the one shown here, had robbed blacks of their rights and privileges.

Fard's religious doctrines and claims to divine authority were called absurd by whites as well as by his black critics, yet they had a great emotional ring of truth to the people who swelled the membership of the Nation of Islam. His followers found his account of the history of mankind to be at least as believable as the one found in the Bible, which was often used by white racists to support their arguments that blacks were inferior. The Nation of Islam, with its message of racial pride and devotion to Allah, hoped to persuade blacks to build a separate society free from the control of whites.

The Nation of Islam's initial period of growth was checked in 1934, when Fard disappeared without a trace. In the aftermath of this mysterious occurrence, Elijah Muhammad became engaged in a battle with other ministers for control of the Nation of Islam. Jailed for three years after being convicted of draft evasion, he eventually gained leadership of the Nation of Islam. As news of his uplifting sermons spread by word of mouth through the black ghettos of Midwestern cities, his stature grew. To his devoted followers, Muhammad was known as "the Messenger," the man who would lead the faithful to the Kingdom of Allah. To Malcolm Little in Norfolk Prison, he seemed to be the man who could free him from his troubled past.

By late 1949, Malcolm had resolved the inner struggles that had propelled him both toward and away from Islam. Describing the tremendous impact that his conversion to Islam had on him, he said, "Every instinct of the ghetto jungle streets, every hustling fox and criminal wolf instinct in me, which would have scoffed at and rejected anything else, was struck numb." He compared his own experience with that of the apostle Paul, who had a similarly blinding revelation when he had converted to Christianity.

When Malcolm told his brothers and sisters that he had accepted Allah, they urged him to write immediately to Elijah Muhammad. It took him more than 25 attempts to write a letter that expressed exactly how he felt about his newfound faith. When he at last finished a draft that satisfied him, he mailed it off. Muhammad answered him promptly, welcoming Malcolm to the knowledge of Islam and telling him to have courage. Following the Nation of Islam's custom, 24-year-old Malcolm dropped his surname and replaced it with the letter *X*.

Having once been a hustler, a drug-dealer, and a thief, Malcolm now set himself on a course to become an active minister of the Nation of Islam and a committed fighter for black freedom and dignity. His ministry and his battle would have to begin, however, while he was still in prison.

RESEARCH PROJECT

The CIA World Factbook website (https://www.cia.gov/library/publications/the-world-factbook) has population and religious adherence figures for all nations. Print out a large map of the world, and note the number of Muslims living in each country. What countries have the largest number of Muslims? Why? Do research in your school library or the Internet to support your conclusions.

TEXT-DEPENDENT QUESTIONS

1. What was Malcolm Little's nickname when he was in Charlestown State Prison?
2. What inmate inspired Malcolm to improve his mind by studying in the prison library?
3. What were some differences between Norfolk State Prison Colony and Charlestown State Prison?
4. What two Nation of Islam teachings stuck in Malcolm's mind after his prison meeting with his brother Reginald?
5. Who founded the Nation of Islam?
6. Who was Elijah Muhammad?

Malcolm X's initial success in drawing converts to the Nation of Islam took place in the black slums of Detroit, the hometown of many of his brothers and sisters.

WORDS TO UNDERSTAND

extramarital relationship—sexual intercourse involving a person who is married and someone who is not that person's spouse.
promiscuity—having sexual relations with several different partners on a casual basis.
vestige—a trace of something that is disappearing or no longer exists.

CHAPTER 5

NATION OF ISLAM

Armed with a militant new spiritual faith, Malcolm X began to search for his place within the Nation of Islam. He was amazed at how quickly his old habits and ways of thinking faded away, but some changes occurred only after a hard struggle. One of his most difficult tasks was learning how to pray in the Islamic fashion, humbly touching his head to the ground while kneeling in the direction of Mecca. "Picking a lock to rob someone's house was the only way my knees had been bent before," he said. Once he became comfortable with praying, however, he felt that another **vestige** of his past life had been swept away.

With Malcolm X's new religious beliefs came an even greater personal commitment to improving his mind. By the beginning of 1950, the reading program he had begun before his conversion to Islam had been in progress for a year. Yet he was still dissatisfied with his handwriting and vocabulary. Determined to correct this weakness, he sat down at the desk in his room and began laboriously copying the first page of a dictionary. It took him all day to finish the task. He copied another page from the dictionary on the following day—and on every day thereafter for the next four years. By following this regimen, he not only improved his handwriting and vocabulary, but also trained himself to exercise self-discipline.

Malcolm X's strict adherence to his writing program was in keeping with the practices of the Nation of Islam. Mental, spiritual, and moral discipline are the great underlying strengths of the religion. Besides maintaining a careful and restricted diet, Black Muslims are required to be neatly dressed, well spoken, and respectful of others, especially other Muslims. Sexual **promiscuity** is strictly forbidden. No practitioner is allowed to drink alcohol or smoke cigarettes.

Malcolm X firmly followed all the Nation of Islam's strictures while making use of his growing skill as a writer. He sent letters to former underworld friends, urging them to follow in his footsteps, and to government officials about the need to fight racial injustice. Writing these letters helped him sort out the benefits of Islam for black Americans and fired his desire to bring the word of Allah to others. He wrote daily to his family in Michigan as well as to Elijah Muhammad about the progress he was making in understanding the teachings of Islam, and the two men built up a steady correspondence.

Malcolm X also engaged in a wide-ranging reading program. Every evening, he pored through books from the Norfolk prison library. After the lights in his room were turned off at 10 P.M., he would read by the light from the hallway. He usually read until 3 A.M., jumping into bed whenever the guards came by on their routine checks, then returning to his book after they had passed. "The ability to read," he said, "awoke in me some long dormant craving to be mentally alive."

Malcolm X began a comprehensive study of history, archaeology, religion, philosophy, and science. His readings included everything from discussions of the theory of genetics to documents about the pre-Civil War antislavery movement. Always reading with an eye for political content, he searched for examples of how the native populations of countries in Asia, Africa, and the Americas were exploited by foreign white rulers and how these peoples had built revolutionary movements to fight for their independence.

A statue of Jomo Kenyatta in Nairobi. The leader of Kenya's struggle for independence from Great Britain in the 1950s, Kenyatta was one of the African freedom fighters who inspired Malcolm X's interest in revolutionary politics.

CHAPTER 5: NATION OF ISLAM

W.E.B. DU BOIS

While in prison, Malcolm X read *The Souls of Black Folk* by W.E.B. Du Bois, published in 1903. The forceful writing impressed Malcolm X, who agreed with Du Bois's strong stand in support of those who actively demanded equal rights.

William Edward Burghardt Du Bois was born in 1868 in Massachusetts. He was an avid student, and, unlike many other African Americans of his time, was able to achieve his dream of higher education. He graduated from Fisk University before becoming the first African American to earn a Ph.D. from Harvard. He then spent two years studying at the University of Berlin in Germany.

Du Bois returned to America impressed by the greater racial tolerance he had experienced while in Germany and determined to change the status of African Americans in his native country. He founded the Niagara Movement with other African-American leaders who shared his determination to bring about racial equality and later became active in the newly founded

Two works that had a strong impact on Malcolm X and opened his eyes to the vast sweep of black American history were W.E.B. Du Bois's book *Souls of Black Folk* and Carter G. Woodson's *Journal of Negro History*. From these and other sources, he learned about the ancient civilizations of Africa and about the enslavement of Africans by the Europeans. He also read about people who resisted slavery, including Nat Turner and other American slave revolt leaders. They provided him with powerful examples of black militancy.

The more Malcolm X read, the more he was able to find personal insights that helped him understand the teachings of Elijah Muhammad. He had only

National Association for the Advancement of Colored People (NAACP), the only African American chosen to serve on the organization's first board of directors. For many years, Du Bois served as editor of the NAACP's magazine, *The Crisis,* and his passionate editorials and strong editorial positions in the magazine often forced a more activist stance for the organization.

Du Bois wrote extensively on the experiences and attitudes of African Americans. He fought bitterly with Booker T. Washington, who Du Bois believed was accommodating racist attitudes rather than trying to create change.

Du Bois was one of the foremost intellectuals of the civil rights movement. Unlike many of his contemporaries in the civil rights movement, he was highly educated, was not religious, and benefited from having many supportive white contacts and mentors.

Du Bois gradually grew disillusioned with the possibility of achieving change in the United States. He moved to Africa, revoking his American citizenship, and became a citizen of Ghana shortly before his death in 1963.

to think back to the one-paragraph summary of black history printed in the textbooks used by his junior high school classes to be reminded of Muhammad's statement that America had "whitened" its own history. The textbooks barely mentioned the horrors of the African slave trade and ignored the considerable achievements of black Americans—subjects that were highlighted in the Nation of Islam's teachings.

As he filled in the gaps in his knowledge, Malcolm X became increasingly confident he had the intellectual gifts necessary to be an effective preacher for the Nation of Islam. He spent less time in his room, took a more active role in prison activities, and engaged in formal debates with other inmates. Gradually, he drew other black prisoners into discussions about the teachings of the Nation of Islam. His fellow inmates were amazed at his change from a God-hating fanatic to an equally zealous preacher for Islam. Nevertheless, some of them began to listen to him.

Malcolm X was well suited for his role as a prison preacher. He knew how to speak to black prisoners: He was one of them. A product of the black ghettos (as were most of the inmates), he knew what kinds of statements would catch their attention. By skillfully mixing talk about the past glories of African civilizations with attacks on America's white-dominated institutions, he was able to interest a number of prisoners in the teachings of the Nation. As he wrote later, "The 'white man is the devil' is the perfect echo of that black convict's lifelong experience."

Malcolm X suffered a great shock when Elijah Muhammad expelled his brother Reginald from the Nation because it was discovered that he was having an **extramarital relationship** with a female member of the Nation. The prison preacher grew even more troubled when Reginald visited him in prison after the expulsion and made a number of charges against Muhammad and the manner in which he was operating the Nation. Malcolm X realized that his loyalties were being severely tested. One man had introduced him to Islam; the other man was his spiritual adviser.

Hoping to patch up the rift between Reginald and the Nation, Malcolm X wrote a letter to Muhammad in which he defended his brother and asked for forgiveness. The following night, he experienced a vision in his prison cell. As he lay in his bed, a man with light brown skin and Asiatic features appeared before him and seated himself on a chair. The man looked at the inmate for a while and then disappeared. Malcolm X believed that the man was W. D. Fard, and his presence meant the troubled prisoner should remain utterly faithful to the Nation.

Muhammad stated in his response to Malcolm X's letter that the correct decision had been made about Reginald, and he counseled his follower to accept the verdict

After converting to Islam, Malcolm X made a commitment to improving his mind by reading voraciously and practicing his writing. He evolved from a violent, rebellious person into someone introspective and charismatic. Prison authorities noticed this change and granted him parole in 1952 after he had served six years.

and go on with his studies. "If you once believed the truth, and now you are beginning to doubt the truth," Muhammad wrote, "then you didn't believe the truth in the first place." Muhammad's stand on the matter was an inflexible one, but it left Malcolm X reassured. There was only one truth, and he would follow it. His brother would have to make his own separate peace with the Nation of Islam.

The improvement in Malcolm X's character after his conversion to Islam was duly noted by prison authorities. In August 1952, at the age of 27, he was released from the penitentiary. He had served six years of his ten-year sentence.

One of the conditions of Malcolm X's parole was that he have a job waiting for him. His brother Wilfred, who was the manager of a furniture business in Detroit, arranged for him to work at the store. "I never looked back," he said after walking past the prison gates.

FISHING FOR ALLAH

Malcolm X's first purchases outside of prison—a pair of eyeglasses, a suitcase, and a wristwatch—were necessities that also had great symbolic importance attached to them. He needed glasses because he had damaged his eyes by reading in poor light, yet he felt they were fitting for someone who had a new focus on life. Sensing that he might be traveling frequently in the years ahead, he believed his new suitcase would become his constant companion.

The decision to wear a watch was perhaps the most telling sign of the radical change in Malcolm X's personality. In his days as a hustler, he had sometimes worn an expensive, flashy watch for show. When he was released from prison, the watch became a symbol for him of time ticking away. The gravity of his mission to spread the word about the Nation weighed on him, and he knew that winning converts in the black ghettos would not be an easy task. Too many years of his life had been wasted, and he was obsessed with the need to work fast.

After having his hair cropped short in the Black Muslim style, Malcolm X left Boston immediately after his release from prison and traveled to his brother Wilfred's house in Detroit. "The warmth of a home and a family was a healing change from the prison cage for me," he said. "It would deeply move almost any newly freed convict, I think. But especially this Muslim home's atmosphere sent me often to my knees to praise Allah."

Malcolm X worked as a furniture salesman in the store that Wilfred managed, and the business practices of the store's white owners, who sold low-quality furniture to black ghetto dwellers on credit at exorbitant interest rates, gave the new employee further insights into the ways in which the poor were exploited. The store owners masked their involvement in the store by hiring black managers and salesmen, and they knew that their poorly educated customers would be unable to read the fine print about high interest rates in the sales agreements. The exploitative practices enraged Malcolm X, who wrote, "I watched brothers entwining themselves in the economic clutches of the white man who went home

Scan here to learn more about Carter G. Woodson:

CHAPTER 5: NATION OF ISLAM

Elijah Muhammad addresses a Nation of Islam assembly.

every night with another bag of money drained from the ghetto." He soon left the furniture store to work in an automobile factory.

Although Malcolm X found little satisfaction in his work, he was nearly ecstatic to be within the welcoming fellowship of the Nation of Islam community in Detroit. He plunged into the group's activities at rituals at Temple Number One, the first mosque to have been established by Fard and Elijah Muhammad. Malcolm X was deeply impressed by the dignity and love he found both in his brother's home and at the temple. The community members exuded a radiant spirit that was much different from the feelings he had found elsewhere. He wrote, "I had never dreamed of anything like that atmosphere among black people who had learned to be proud they were black." During this period, the Nation of Islam's recruiting efforts had been meeting with only moderate success. Malcolm X was surprised that the temple usually had many empty seats at its prayer meetings. Nearly bursting with pride in his newfound faith, he could not believe that more blacks did not jump to embrace the Nation's message. He realized that a much more effective recruiting campaign was needed to get the word of Allah to the people.

Shortly after he arrived in Michigan, Malcolm X had his first meeting with Elijah Muhammad, the man whom he revered for saving him from a life of crime and despair. Malcolm X visited the Messenger at his home in Chicago and was almost overcome with his feelings of awe for the gentle, fatherly man. When they began to discuss the Nation of Islam, Malcolm X could not help voicing his disappointment about the lack of active members in the Detroit temple. Muhammad, sensing the young convert's dynamism, agreed with his observation. "Go after the young people," Muhammad instructed. "Once you get them the older ones will follow."

Taking the Messenger's advice to heart, Malcolm X went "fishing," the term that Black Muslims used for their recruiting expeditions. He made circuits of Detroit's pool halls, barrooms, and street corners, engaging young men with a bit of opening ghetto slang to get their attention: "My man, let me pull your coat on something." Many people shied away from him as if he were a crazy man. Others listened spellbound as he talked about the power and beauty of the black race and of how Allah was soon going to sweep the white man from the face of the earth.

Malcolm X would speak until he was hoarse, and afterwards he would pace the streets for hours, brooding about ways to reach the souls of black Americans who would not listen to him. They were people whose hair was conked, who sought to deny their black heritage, and who were destroying themselves with drugs and alcohol. These men and women reminded him of his own past, and he vowed to help them find the same strong spiritual faith that he had found.

Within a few months, Malcolm X almost single-handedly tripled the membership of Temple Number One. By mixing his attacks on whites with humorous analogies that urged his listeners to stop imitating their white oppressors and stop depending on white charities, he won them over. "The man who tosses worms in the river isn't necessarily a friend of the fish," he told his audiences. "All the fish who took him for a friend, who think the worm's got no hooks in it, usually end up on the frying pan."

By luring recruits with sharp words and a barbed wit, Malcolm X apparently had the most effective hooks of all.

RESEARCH PROJECT

Using the internet or your school library, research the life and teachings of Elijah Muhammad. Write a two-page report and share it with your class.

TEXT-DEPENDENT QUESTIONS

1. How did Malcolm improve his handwriting and vocabulary?
2. What were two books that had a strong impact on Malcolm while he was in prison?
3. Why was Malcolm an effective prison preacher?
4. Where did Malcolm go after he was released from prison on parole?

The Messenger—Elijah Muhammad—speaks at a Nation of Islam rally. During the 1950s, the Nation of Islam's open defiance of white authority attracted huge crowds to the organization's rallies in support of black unity.

WORDS TO UNDERSTAND

apocalypse—the end of the world, or an event that causes significant damage and destruction.

conscientious objector—a person who refuses to serve in the armed forces or carry a weapon due to his moral or religious beliefs.

subordinate—a person who is under the control of someone else within an organization, or is treated as being of lower rank or less importance.

CHAPTER 6

THE LEADER OF TEMPLE NUMBER SEVEN

Malcolm X's success in filling the benches of the Nation of Islam's Detroit temple earned him an appointment as assistant minister there in 1953. Burning with religious and political fervor, he decided to quit his job at the automobile factory and devote all his time to missionary work. He traveled frequently to Chicago to speak with Elijah Muhammad and study at the library in the Messenger's home.

More and more, Muhammad looked on Malcolm X as his star pupil. He was a natural leader, with magnetic charm and an aura of spirituality that drew people to the temples. The Nation was having a hard time getting its message to a large audience and strongly needed a preacher who could appeal to the black masses in the cities. Malcolm X seemed to Muhammad like the perfect choice.

In 1953, Muhammad gave Malcolm X his first major assignment: Organize a temple in Boston. Before he could leave Detroit, he was visited by FBI agents who questioned him about the Nation and about why he had not registered with his military draft board. With the Korean War in progress, all men over the age of 18 and a half were required to register for service in the armed forces.

Malcolm X went directly to the local draft board and declared himself a **conscientious objector** to service in the military. When asked if he knew the meaning of "conscientious objection," he replied, "When the white man [asks] me to go somewhere and fight and maybe die to preserve the way the white man [treats] the black man in America, then my conscience objects." He received a deferred status and heard nothing more from the army.

Malcolm X began his new ministry in Boston preaching in the living room of a fellow Black Muslim. While in the city, he visited many of his old friends in Roxbury. Quite a few of them were distrustful of his new Islamic beliefs. The "wire," as street gossip was called, was reporting that Malcolm X was on a "religious kick," and his old hustling friends suspected he was operating another of the storefront confidence

In the 1950s Malcolm X took over the leadership of Temple Number Seven, a Nation of Islam mosque in Harlem. Today, the building is a Sunni Muslim mosque known as Masjid Malcolm Shabazz.

To see an archaeological study at Malcolm X's Boston home, scan here:

games that were common throughout the ghetto. Malcolm X realized that his friends were not ready to accept what he was preaching, so he did not attempt to convert them.

Within three months of his arrival in Boston, Malcolm X had organized a thriving Nation of Islam community, which met in its own small temple. Pleased with his minister's success, Muhammad sent him to Philadelphia to establish another temple. Again, Malcolm X quickly gathered a group of converts to Islam. Before long, the Nation had its 12th temple, and Malcolm X was recognized as the group's rising star.

Because of his superb preaching, which he had constantly refined during his "fishing" expeditions, Malcolm X was often referred to as the Nation's "hard hitting young minister." He could preach for hours, and he often did. His message—the word of Elijah Muhammad—was always the same, and it was usually peppered with references to the evil deeds of whites and the coming **apocalypse** that would utterly destroy them.

Malcolm X also preached about the need for blacks to unify and reach out to each other. He told his audiences to feel enraged about the indignities they had to

The Fruit of Islam is the security service for the Nation of Islam. They acted as bodyguards and enforcers for Malcolm X, Elijah Muhammad, and other high-ranking members of the Nation of Islam.

endure at the hands of whites, to liberate themselves from their feelings of self-hatred and worthlessness, and to take pride in their black heritage. Speaking to his temple congregations, he said, "We all have in common the greatest binding tie we could have—we all are black people."

Malcolm accused all white Americans of racism. He held out little hope that their attitude toward blacks would change. The liberties that white Americans prized for themselves, even during the years when slavery was practiced in the United States, would never be fully extended to blacks. "We didn't land on the Plymouth Rock, my brothers and sisters," he said, "Plymouth Rock landed on us!" To get out from under that rock, he preached, blacks must throw off their dependence on whites and build a separate society. In addition, he said, blacks must worship according to the beliefs of their own special religion, the Nation of Islam.

In June 1954, as a reward for his hard work, Malcolm X was appointed to head Temple Number Seven in New York City. The temple was located in the most depressed area of Harlem, yet he was ecstatic about the assignment. He had come full circle. Only ten years before, he had been one of the most deluded and desperate hustlers in the district. Now he returned as a minister, a pure flame of Allah, to ignite a revolution in the largest black community in America.

At first, Malcolm X had trouble getting the Nation's message heard because other groups in Harlem were also preaching that blacks should turn their backs on white society. With his customary energy, though, he traveled through the ghetto's streets and soon began to pull hundreds of new converts into the Nation. Among his best sources for recruits were the small, storefront Christian churches that lined the streets of Harlem's poorest areas. He and his assistants waited until the church services were over and then pounced on the congregants with the message that Christianity was a slave master's religion. After listening to him preach, many former Baptists and Catholics became devout Muslims.

Temple Number Seven grew quickly, but not swiftly enough for Malcolm X. Besides preaching six or seven nights a week at temple meetings and on Harlem street corners, he organized a nightly adult education course, during which he led debates about current events and religious topics. He also found the time to preach regularly in Philadelphia and logged many miles on the road as he drove to Springfield, Massachusetts; Hartford, Connecticut; and Atlanta, Georgia, to organize new temples.

By 1957, Malcolm X was traveling to the West Coast and starting temples in Los Angeles and other western cities. He ultimately had a hand in the formation of more than two dozen new congregations throughout the country. By the end of the 1950s, the Nation became a formidable presence in the ghettos of the nation's biggest cities thanks largely to his inexhaustible energy.

Malcolm X's primary assistant in leading Temple Number Seven was Joseph X (formerly Joseph Gravitt of Detroit). Known as "Captain Joseph," he rose to a leadership position in the Nation of Islam, eventually becoming director of the Fruit of Islam.

FRUIT OF ISLAM

The Nation was a relatively poor organization whose members often lived from hand to mouth during the mid-1950s. Gradually, however, the Nation's financial situation changed as its membership grew, for all members were required to make substantial monetary contributions to the organization. The group began to buy real estate and start small businesses. Some members ran farms, while others operated bakeries, clothing stores, and even small factories. The profits from these business ventures helped the Nation expand its ministry and build a large temple headquarters in Chicago.

The membership of the Nation, which in the group's early years had been drawn mainly from the poorest blacks and reformed convicts such as Malcolm X, began to include converts from the educated middle class. The adult males of each of the Nation's temples composed a tightly organized corps known as the Fruit of Islam, and they attended weekly sessions to receive instruction in religious doctrine, moral issues, and self-defense techniques. The female members of the Nation, known as the Muslim Sisters, were held in great respect, but were expected to play a **subordinate** role to the men.

The Nation's strict moral code and the iron discipline it exerted over its members frightened away some potential converts. Yet when Malcolm X was recruiting, he used these aspects of the organization to his advantage. He told ghetto residents that whites preferred blacks to remain disorganized, lazy, and demoralized because then they were easier to control. He often directed his message at the silent black masses in urban slums, hoping to harness their rage for a holy war against the "blue-eyed devils."

Malcolm X did not use just angry words to stir up his audiences. He also encouraged them to focus a rational eye on their situations and find clearheaded solutions to their problems. He referred to this process of breaking down complex issues as "cracking atoms," and he often used this line of deductive reasoning to demonstrate the methods by which blacks were forced to remain second-class citizens.

As the recruiting efforts of Malcolm X and other Black Muslim ministers became increasingly successful, the organization began to hold national meetings. Members from around the country gathered in Chicago every year on Savior's Day, February 26, to celebrate the birthday of W. D. Fard. The Nation also staged huge rallies, known as Living Fountain assemblies, in many cities. Malcolm X was the organizing force behind these gatherings, and his dynamic speaking presence often overshadowed the official focus of the assemblies: Elijah Muhammad, the Living Fountain.

The Nation's growth in the 1950s occurred at a time when enormous changes seemed to be in store for race relations in the United States. While Malcolm X was delivering his black separatist message to audiences in the ghettos, a young minister named Martin Luther King, Jr., was leading a boycott of segregated bus services in Montgomery, Alabama. Throughout the South, civil rights organizations, such as the Southern Christian Leadership Conference (SCLC) and the Congress on Racial Equality (CORE), were challenging racial segregation in public schools and theaters, in restaurants and rest rooms, on trains and buses. Although the nonviolent protest marches led by King and his colleagues often met with brutal retaliation from white policemen and white supremacist organizations, the civil rights movement was beginning to have some success in eroding racial discrimination in the South.

The civil rights marchers won much praise for their courageous fight for racial integration, but not from Malcolm X. He had nothing but contempt for their goals and tactics. "You can sit down next to white folks—on the toilet," he remarked, belittling recent rulings outlawing segregated rest rooms. He told those who championed integration, "The masses of black people want a society

An African-American woman is carried to a police wagon in Brooklyn during a civil-rights demonstration. Malcolm X was opposed to the nonviolent civil disobedience of mainstream civil rights groups, and called for blacks to defend themselves if attacked.

CHAPTER 6: THE LEADER OF TEMPLE NUMBER SEVEN 85

A crowd of Black Muslims applauds during the annual Savior's Day message in Chicago.

of their own in a land of their own." Criticizing nonviolent protest methods that required blacks to sacrifice their bodies and sometimes their lives in fighting for their constitutional rights, he called for blacks to defend themselves when attacked—bullet for bullet, if necessary.

By 1957, Malcolm X's militant ideas had begun to attract some fervent advocates in the Northern black ghettos. The Nation's membership numbered around 1,000 at this time, and he was able to call on a cadre of 60 or 70 hard-core Muslim activists for rallies that he held in the streets of Harlem. The New York Police Department, which kept tabs on groups deemed to be potentially troublesome, had files on some of the Black Muslims. Many of the city's leaders, though—even some of its black ones—had never heard of the group. That all changed one April evening in 1957.

That night, on a Harlem street, the police broke up a fight. While making their arrests, the police brusquely ordered the bystanders to move on. Several members of Temple Number Seven were among those watching the incident, and they refused to move. They wanted to make sure that the men who had just been arrested would not be beaten by the police. Angered by the Muslims' obstinacy, the police attacked one of them, a man named Hinton Johnson, and opened up a large gash in his scalp. He was then arrested and taken to police precinct headquarters, where he was thrown into a cell.

Less than an hour later, 50 members of the Fruit of Islam, with Malcolm X at the head of the group, stood in military formation outside the precinct house where Johnson was being held. They remained absolutely silent and created an eerie scene that was part confrontation and part vigil. Their defiant stance quickly attracted a large crowd of onlookers.

Harlem had been the site of many riots and murders before, but its residents had never witnessed a show of defiance and solidarity quite like this one. Blacks were not in the habit of directly confronting the police. In fact, the police were also drawn to the display and came to the windows of the precinct building to stare at the Black Muslims.

Finally, Malcolm X went into the precinct house and demanded to see Johnson. At first, the police refused to let him see the beaten man, but they were getting nervous because of the growing crowd outside, and they finally gave in to Malcolm's request.

As soon as Malcolm X saw the condition Johnson was in, he demanded that the badly injured man be taken to Harlem Hospital. An angry crowd followed the ambulance to the hospital and waited outside until they heard that Johnson was receiving proper medical care. Upon being told that the injured man was being treated, Malcolm X made a gesture to the crowd, and the people instantly dispersed.

One white policeman who was at the scene was heard to say, "This is too much power for one man to have."

The Johnson incident made headlines not only in New York's leading black newspaper, the *Amsterdam News*, but also in the city's major dailies. With their show of strength outside the station house, the Black Muslims were letting the Harlem community know that the relationship between its police force and its inhabitants was changing. Harlemites started to look upon Malcolm X and the Nation of Islam with awe, a feeling that increased when Johnson and the Nation sued the police and won a large settlement. By then, the Black Muslims were a force to be reckoned with in Harlem. Politicians and community leaders thought it best not to make any critical statements that would spark a mass impromptu street rally of the group and its supporters.

Malcolm's voice was rapidly becoming the most feared—and perhaps the best loved—in Harlem. Yet he knew there was a much larger theater waiting. The nationwide struggle against racial oppression was just heating up, and he was burning to be a part of it. Calling out to black Americans to throw off the shackles of passivity and self-deprecation, he preached, "My black brothers and sisters—no one will know who we are ... until we know who we are."

Malcolm X wanted to be known as more than an outspoken preacher. If he became a spokesman of the frustration and anger of ghetto blacks, though, he would be taking on a difficult—and dangerous—role.

RESEARCH PROJECT

During the 1950s and 1960s, black Americans who were angry about their living conditions rioted in a number of major cities, including New York, Washington, D.C., Chicago, Los Angeles, and Newark, New Jersey. Find out more about one of these riots. How did it begin? What was the extent of the damage? How was the rioting finally ended? Write a two-page report and share it with your class.

TEXT-DEPENDENT QUESTIONS

1. What was Malcolm X's first major assignment with the Nation of Islam, in 1953?
2. Where was Temple Number Seven located?
3. What did Malcolm X think about nonviolent protests?
4. Who was Hinton Johnson?

Stating that blacks could not afford to wait any longer for racial justice to be won, Malcolm X excited crowds in northern ghettos by calling for an immediate black revolt against white power.

WORDS TO UNDERSTAND

civil disobedience—refusal to comply with certain laws that are considered unfair, as a peaceful form of political protest.

demagogue— a political leader who appeals to popular prejudices and makes false promises in order to gain power.

usurp—to take and hold a position of authority without the right to do so.

CHAPTER 7

HUSBAND, FATHER, FIGHTER

At the age of 34, Malcolm X emerged as an extremely important figure in the Nation of Islam's affairs. Elijah Muhammad was suffering from bronchial asthma, so Malcolm X toured Africa in 1959 as the organization's ambassador and established relations with Muslim groups in Egypt and other countries on the African continent. Newspaper and television reporters anxious to hear the Nation's opinion on developments in racial relations in the United States began seeking him out, and he was ready and willing to serve as the group's sharp-tongued spokesman.

The Nation had emerged from relative obscurity at a time when racial discrimination was one of the most hotly debated issues in America. Malcolm X, Elijah Muhammad, and the Nation became especially visible after being featured on "The Hate That Hate Produced," a television documentary that aired in 1959. Narrated by journalist Mike Wallace, the program showed how violently the Black Muslims and their supporters resented white society and was filled with graphic evidence that a firestorm was gathering in the country's black ghettos. It was a shocking revelation to most white Americans, who had no inkling that discontent among blacks ran so deep.

> Malcolm X's wife had been born Betty Dean Sanders before she joined the Nation of Islam in 1956 and changed her name to Betty X, to represent renunciation of her "slave name." They were married in 1958 and had six daughters.

Looking to further publicize the Nation's views, Malcolm X started publishing a newspaper, *Muhammad Speaks*, in the basement of his home. This weekly periodical, which printed the sayings of Elijah Muhammad along with relentless attacks on white racism, was an immediate success in the black community and eventually became the largest-circulating black publication in the country, with a circulation of more than a half million. The papers were sold by the members of the Fruit of Islam.

At the helm of Temple Number Seven, Malcolm X remained a study in contrasts. Always neatly dressed in a dark suit and narrow tie, he hardly looked the part of a ghetto warrior. His speech combined the latest street slang with his now-vast vocabulary. He thrived on highly emotional appeals to his audience, yet he was also known for having a cool head, logical thoughts, and an unshakable nerve. Some people found him aloof, cynical, and combative; others were impressed by his deep love for the black race and the compassion he showed for the poor and homeless.

Malcolm X's character had taken a turn in 1958, when he married Betty X (later known as Betty Shabazz), a nurse and teacher at the Nation's New York temple. The marriage startled his friends because he had never hesitated to express his deep distrust of women—though he always said women should be treated with respect. Yet he clearly trusted Betty, an understanding, supportive wife who knew that the black struggle came first in her husband's life.

Malcolm and Betty's first child, Attilah, was born in 1958. They eventually had five more daughters: Quibilah, Ilyasah, Gamilah, Malaak, and Malikah. A loving husband and father, he regretted that his hectic schedule often took him away from his family for weeks at a time. He treasured the moments they spent together at their home in East Elmhurst, located in the New York City borough of Queens.

To see Malcolm X speak at a Harlem rally, scan here:

LOUIS FARRAKHAN

In the 1960s, Malcolm X's fiery speeches were echoed by the lyrics of a young calypso singer who had joined the Nation of Islam. He recorded a song, "A White Man's Heaven is a Black Man's Hell"; changed his name first to Louis X and then to Louis Farrakhan; and became one of the most controversial leaders of the Nation of Islam.

Farrakhan was born in New York on May 11, 1933. He attended Winston-Salem Teachers College before working as a calypso singer. In 1955, he joined the Nation of Islam, ultimately moving to New York to work with Elijah Muhammad and Malcolm X. When Malcolm X left the Nation of Islam in 1964, Farrakhan replaced him as minister of Mosque Number Seven in Harlem.

A split in the membership of the Nation of Islam occurred with the death of Elijah Muhammad in 1975. Farrakhan served as head of the Nation of Islam, and Muhammad's son formed a new group, known as the Muslim American Community.

Farrakhan has become a controversial, if highly visible, leader of the Nation of Islam. Many of his speeches have been marked by rhetoric

---

The living conditions in Harlem were such that Malcolm X was unwilling to raise a family there, yet the ghetto remained the focus of his life. The anger he felt as he looked at the broken homes and heard the despairing voices gave him the strength of spirit he needed to campaign on behalf of the powerless and forgotten people of the black ghettos. Other black American leaders may have been heartened by the sight of the civil rights marches in the South, but Malcolm X refused to feel optimistic about the nation's slow progress in improving racial considered racist, sexist, and anti-Semitic. In 1983, Farrakhan supported Jesse Jackson during his campaign for the presidency, often appearing with Jackson at campaign rallies and speeches, until his anti-Semitic comments began to cause problems for the Jackson campaign. Farrakhan ultimately was asked to leave the Jackson campaign, and Jackson was forced to publicly distance himself from the controversial leader.

In 1995, Qubilah Shabazz, the daughter of Malcolm X, was accused of plotting to murder Farrakhan following her mother's public accusation that Farrakhan was involved in Malcolm X's assassination. In that same year, Farrakhan organized the Million Man March, a highly successful gathering of hundreds of thousands of African-American men in Washington. The march's stated aim—to unify a million "committed, dedicated, inspired black men for a day of atonement"—was extremely popular, but Farrakhan's speeches alienated as many as the march attracted.

Farrakhan remains leader of the Nation of Islam, although since the mid-2000s he has relinquished some of his public duties due to health issues.

relations. "The black masses are living a nightmare," he insisted.

Malcolm X's greatest hope was to foster a black revolution. Crowds of his supporters held rallies on Harlem's Lenox Avenue (later renamed Malcolm X Avenue) and heard him demand that America live up to its promise of freedom and justice for its black citizens. "White people," he said, "need someone to tell them what time it is." His view was that there was only one solution to the country's racial problems: Black Americans must unite and form a separate nation, either within the United

States or in Africa. Until blacks lived free from white domination, he said, America would not have any peace.

The 1960s began with Malcolm X continuing to dream of a revolution that would produce a separate nation for blacks. At the same time, a new force was taking hold of the civil rights movement: activist groups such as the Student Nonviolent Coordinating Committee (SNCC), formed by many of the young people who had marched with Martin Luther King, Jr., in Montgomery. Although they still believed in King's tactics of nonviolent **civil disobedience**, the students turned to more confrontational methods to protest against segregation and racial violence in the South. Their aggressive protest actions helped to boost black pride throughout the country, and Malcolm X welcomed their aggressive spirit.

As the 1960s progressed, sweeping changes in the nation's racial attitudes failed to materialize, and the high hopes of the civil rights marchers from the 1950s began to wane. More and more blacks, especially young blacks in the Northern ghettos, started to share Malcolm X's view that the campaign of nonviolent resistance was yielding minimal results. His supporters could be heard humming "White Man's Heaven Is a Black Man's Hell," a popular song recorded by Louis X (today known as Louis Farrakhan), a former calypso singer who had become the minister of the Nation's Boston temple.

Thousands of militant young blacks flocked to hear Malcolm X's radical message. Journalists hounded him for his opinions about America's race relations, and he obliged them with his usual controversial statements. Styling himself as the uncompromising champion of the black masses, he was relentless in attacking any social program that stopped short of demanding black liberation. When white leaders told him to be patient, he answered that blacks had waited long enough for compensation, and added an ominous warning: We do not forget, we do not forgive.

Malcolm X thrived on battling verbally with his critics. They accused him of being a violent revolutionary, an extremist, a **demagogue** who used emotionalism

Malcolm X and his family lived in this home in Queens borough of New York City.

to obscure the issues, a hatemonger who was stirring up bad blood between whites and blacks. He responded that he was engaged in a war to free blacks from the misguided policies of more moderate black leaders, whom he scathingly described as "men with black bodies and white heads." He ridiculed anyone who believed the American government would agree to major racial reforms without the threat of a massive black uprising. Revolutions, he noted pointedly, are rarely bloodless.

Even though he called for blacks to denounce whites, Malcolm X was uncomfortable being depicted as a man who preached hate. He saw himself as someone who was seeking to promote unity among Muslims and blacks, not as a violent

Leaders of two diametrically opposed wings of the black activist movement, Malcolm X and civil rights leader Martin Luther King Jr., waged an often bitter contest for the loyalties of black Americans. Malcolm X sharply criticized King's nonviolent protest tactics and his support for integration.

fanatic. Yet when he was questioned about his views, he often gave blunt answers that offended many people, both black and white. He believed there is no such thing as "bad" publicity and used the media to spread his reputation.

Malcolm X's confrontational manner made him a tremendous success as a public speaker. Audiences enjoyed his abrasive style so much that he became one of the most popular speakers on the college lecture circuit. There he discovered that many white students applauded his efforts and seemed to be genuinely committed to solving the country's racial problems. He held out the hope that the younger generation would not repeat the mistakes of their elders.

A RIFT FORMS

In 1962, with Elijah Muhammad still plagued by poor health, Malcolm X was appointed the national minister of the Nation of Islam. In this role, he was officially recognized as acting prime minister for Muhammad and heir apparent to the group's leadership. His appointment, however, aroused the jealousy of other Black Muslims—among them John Ali—who wanted to head the Nation, and Malcolm X soon began to suspect his rivals were turning Muhammad against him.

Initially, all Malcolm X heard were rumors that he was trying to **usurp** power from Muhammad. Then his name and picture began to appear less frequently in *Muhammad Speaks*, the editing and production of which had been taken away from him and reassigned to the Nation's headquarters in Chicago. Next, he was told by Muhammad to decline all invitations to appear on prominent television news broadcasts. Clearly, a rift was forming between the Messenger and his onetime favorite minister.

Events in the larger political arena were also troubling Malcolm X at this time. In April 1962, a confrontation between Black Muslims and police in Los Angeles left one group member dead and a dozen others wounded. Malcolm X wanted to retaliate by attacking the police, but the Nation's other leaders were unwilling to risk further trouble and forbade him to do anything more than make angry speeches. He perceived this as a weak response and believed many people would begin to question whether the Black Muslims deserved their militant reputation.

As the infighting continued, Malcolm X remained the heart and soul of militant black resistance for many ghetto dwellers even though he was on bad terms with the majority of the mainstream black leaders. In August 1963, when more than 200,000 people gathered in Washington, D.C., to sing hymns and march in support of racial understanding and greater civil rights legislation, he watched the demonstration from the sidelines and called the march a wasted effort. He told reporters, "I don't

THE MARCH ON WASHINGTON

On August 28, 1963, more than 200,000 supporters of civil rights—most of them African Americans—gathered on the National Mall in Washington, D.C. The event, dubbed the March on Washington for Jobs and Freedom, was organized by the leaders of six groups representing blacks. The goal was to put pressure on the Kennedy administration and the U.S. Congress to pass civil rights legislation.

One of the highlights of the March on Washington was Martin Luther King's famous "I Have a Dream" speech. From the steps of the Lincoln Memorial, King spelled out his vision of an America in which his "four little children will one day live in a nation where they will not be judged by the color of their skin but by the content of their character."

Many people believe that King's speech and the March on Washington were important factors leading to the passage of the Civil Rights Act of 1964, as well as the Voting Rights Act of 1964. These were major pieces of legislation promoting equality for black Americans.

At the time of the March on Washington, however, Malcolm X dismissed it as a big publicity event, dreamed up primarily by white people to make black Americans feel as if they were making progress. He sneeringly referred to it as "the Farce on Washington."

believe we're going to overcome [by] singing. If you're going to get yourself a .45 and start singing 'We Shall Overcome,' I'm with you."

Although Malcolm X was pessimistic about the value of peaceful protest marches, pressure from civil rights groups eventually persuaded Congress to pass a number of major bills outlawing a wide range of racially discriminatory practices. Among them were the Civil Rights Act of 1964 and the Economic Opportunity Act. Yet he continued to insist that the new laws were only showpieces and would not lead to any substantial improvements for blacks. "You don't stick a knife in a man's back nine inches and pull it out six inches and say you're making progress," he argued. Black America was still seething, according to him, and he pointed to recent outbreaks of racial violence in Northern cities as signs that the ghettos were about to erupt.

Malcolm X's fiery speeches denouncing an American society dominated by whites made him a popular, if controversial, public speaker. On November 19, 1963, in Detroit, Michigan, he delivered his "Message to the Grass Roots" speech, in which he reminded his audience:

You are nothing but a ex-slave. You don't like to be told that. But what else are you? You are ex-slaves. You didn't come here on the Mayflower. You came here on a slave ship—in chains, like a horse, or a cow, or a chicken. And you were brought here by the people who came here on the Mayflower. You were brought here by the so-called Pilgrims, or Founding Fathers. They were the ones who brought you here.

We have a common enemy. We have this in common: We have a common oppressor, a common exploiter, and a common discriminator. But once we all realize that we have this common enemy, then we unite on the basis of what we have in common. And what we have foremost in common is that enemy—the white man. He's an enemy to all of us. I know some of you all think that some of them aren't enemies. Time will tell.

By the end of 1963, however, Malcolm X had to set aside all thoughts of a revolution as he engaged in a tremendous political battle within the Nation of Islam. He had heard rumors earlier in the year that Elijah Muhammad had fathered four

Los Angeles police arrest a black man in Los Angeles. Malcolm X wanted to escalate a 1962 confrontation between Black Muslims and police, but was prevented from doing so by the Nation of Islam's leaders.

children by two women who were his former secretaries. The women were serving Muhammad with a paternity suit, and Malcolm X found his faith in the Nation greatly shaken because adultery was a grave violation of Muslim ethics. He spoke to Muhammad's two accusers, and they not only provided him with evidence to back up their claims but also told him that Muhammad had predicted that his dynamic chief assistant would someday turn against him.

When Malcolm X confronted Muhammad on the matter, the Messenger did not deny the accusations but justified his actions by comparing himself with such biblical figures as David and Noah, who also had moral lapses. Muhammad's excuse did not satisfy Malcolm X, but there was little he could do about it. The only result of the incident was an increase in his alienation from Muhammad.

Malcolm X's troubles soon grew. On November 22, 1963, President John F. Kennedy was assassinated in Dallas, Texas, and the entire nation deeply mourned the loss of its popular leader. Yet in discussing the tragedy, Malcolm X stated, "the chickens [have] come home to roost"—meaning that whites were being repaid for establishing a climate of violence in America. The comment created an uproar throughout the United States.

Muhammad realized that a convenient time had come to deal with Malcolm X's threat to his leadership. He suspended the national minister from his duties for a period of 90 days. While Malcolm X was faithfully obeying the suspension, he encountered more troubling news: Some Black Muslims were plotting to murder him for his alleged rebellion against the Messenger. He had often received death threats from white hate groups, but it stunned him to hear that his Muslim brothers would conspire to kill him. Shaken by these events, he wrote, "I felt like something in nature had failed—like the sun or the stars."

In January 1964, Muhammad summoned Malcolm X to Chicago to face charges that he was planning a rebellion. Among his accusers at the hearing were his chief rivals within the Nation. Knowing that a decision on the case would not be rendered for several months, Muhammad sent him to New York with the orders, "Go back and put out the fire you started." Otherwise, he was to keep his distance from other members of the Nation.

Malcolm X knew that chance for reconciliation with Muhammad were fading fast. In February 1964, he and his family went to Miami, Florida, to stay with Cassius Clay, a popular black American boxer. Clay had first heard Malcolm X speak in 1962, and had been inspired by Malcolm's depiction of his faith. The two men met soon after, and Malcolm X became a spiritual mentor and role model for Clay, who secretly joined the Nation of Islam. Now, the 22-year-old boxer had asked Malcolm X to stay at his training camp while he prepared for a bout in Miami against the reigning heavyweight champion of the world, Sonny Liston.

Malcolm X hoped Muhammad would approve of the association, which brought a lot of publicity to the Nation of Islam, and reinstate him. On February 25, 1964, Clay defeated Liston in six rounds to become the new heavyweight champion. It was a tremendous upset, as Liston had been favored to win. At a press conference the next day, Clay publicly announced his membership in the Nation of Islam, and announced that he was dropping his "slave name" and would in future be known as Cassius X. (A month later, his name would be changed again, to Muhammad Ali.)

Despite this publicity, the Messenger remained at odds with Malcolm X. A member of Temple Number Seven told Malcolm X upon his return to New York that the Nation's headquarters had sent word he should be killed. The fiery minister believed only one man had the authority to order such an act: Elijah Muhammad. Malcolm X had become so popular in New York that the Messenger's rule there was being jeopardized.

With great anguish, Malcolm X ended his association with the Nation and looked for a new path to follow, although he had little doubt where it would lead. "My life," he said, "was inseparably committed to the American black man's struggle." No matter which direction he took to carry out his continuing quest for a revolution, he knew he would remain true to an earlier vow to "never forget that any wings I wore had been put on by the religion of Islam."

RESEARCH PROJECT

Malcolm X's forceful personality and compelling speaking manner inspired many to become converts to the Nation of Islam. One of the most famous was the boxer Cassius Clay, later known as Muhammad Ali. To get a better understanding of the relationship between Malcolm X and Muhammad Ali, read the National Public Radio article, "Muhammad Ali And Malcolm X: A Broken Friendship, An Enduring Legacy." (Available at www.npr.org/sections/codeswitch/2016/02/25/467247668/muhammad-ali-and-malcolm-x-a-broken-friendship-an-enduring-legacy)

TEXT-DEPENDENT QUESTIONS

1. What was the name of Malcolm X's newspaper?
2. Where did Malcolm X's supporters hold rallies in Harlem?
3. What was the Student Nonviolent Coordinating Committee (SNCC)
4. How did Malcolm X learn that a rift was forming between him and Elijah Muhammad?
5. What was Malcolm X's controversial statement about the assassination of President John F. Kennedy in November 1963?

Though often radical and controversial, Malcolm X was a powerful spokesman who had a keen understanding of the issues of the black community. He is remembered today not only as a black militant, but also as a leader with a thirst for knowledge who was determined to bring justice to his community by any means necessary.

WORDS TO UNDERSTAND

hajj—a pilgrimage to Mecca, during which Muslims participate in a number of rituals and worship services. The *hajj* is a duty that each Sunni Muslim is expected to undertake at least once during his or her lifetime, if the Muslim is healthy enough and can afford to do so.

hypocrite— a person who pretends to have virtues, morals, or religious beliefs that the person does not actually possess.

Qur'an—the holy book of Islam, believed to contain Allah's actual words, as revealed to Muhammad.

Sunni Islam—the majority sect of Muslims, making up about 80 percent of the total worldwide population. Sunnis believe that they are following the proper path that was set out by the Prophet Muhammad and the early Islamic community.

CHAPTER 8

CHALLENGES AND THREATS

Malcolm X announced at a crowded press conference in March 1964 that he was leaving the Nation of Islam to found an organization called Muslim Mosque, Incorporated. It was to be centered in New York City, where a core group of about 50 participants—all former members of the Nation—would act as "the working base for an action program designed to eliminate the political oppression, the economic exploitation, and the social degradation suffered daily by twenty-two million Afro-Americans." He invited blacks of all religious denominations to join the group.

Without spelling out a specific agenda for his new organization, Malcolm X made it clear that Muslim Mosque was to be a revolutionary group. He stated that blacks should seize control of their communities and form armed resistance organizations to protect themselves. "Like Samson," he said, "I am ready to pull down the white man's temple, knowing full well that I will be destroyed by the falling rubble." He was willing, though, to make some uncharacteristic concessions. He was willing to join forces with less radical black leaders. Whites were also welcome to contribute money and ideas.

BETTY SHABAZZ

Betty Shabazz is best known as the wife of Malcolm X, but her efforts on behalf of civil rights continued long after her husband's death.

Betty Shabazz was born Betty Sanders on May 28, 1936, in Detroit, Michigan. She studied at the Tuskegee Institute, a historically black college in Alabama, before moving to New York to work as a nurse. Friends invited her to attend lectures by Elijah Muhammad, and she soon joined the Nation of Islam. She met Malcolm X in 1956, and they married two years later. Within five years, the couple had four daughters.

When Malcolm X left the Nation of Islam in 1964, he and his wife took the Muslim surname Shabazz. Betty and their daughters were in the audience of the Audubon Ballroom in Harlem when Malcolm was assassinated in 1965. At the time, Shabazz was pregnant; later in the year, she gave birth to twin daughters.

Left with little money and a family of six to raise, Shabazz returned to college, first earning a B.A. in public health education from Jersey City State College and later a Ph.D. in education from the University of Massachusetts. She served as an administrator and later as an assistant

---

The news of Malcolm X's organization sent ripples of excitement through Harlem. The leaders of the Nation, however, were enraged and unleashed a savage attack on him. Muslim newspapers branded him a **hypocrite** and traitor. The Nation's lawyers filed suit to reclaim title to Malcolm X's house, and the group's leaders even ordered his brothers Wilfred X and Philbert X to denounce "the traitor" publicly.

CIVIL RIGHTS LEADERS: MALCOLM X

professor at Medgar Evers College in Brooklyn and became a popular speaker, leading discussions on racial tolerance and civil rights.

In a 1994 speech, Shabazz voiced her suspicions (shared by others) that Nation of Islam leader Louis Farrakhan had been involved in the plot to assassinate her husband. A year later, her daughter Qubilah was arrested in Minneapolis, Minnesota, after attempting to hire a hit man to kill Farrakhan. Betty publicly supported her daughter, insisting that she was the victim of entrapment. Charges were dropped after Qubilah agreed to undergo treatment for alcohol abuse and psychiatric problems.

Shabazz later reconciled with Farrakhan, meeting with him during a fundraiser for her daughter's defense. In 1995, she spoke at the Million Man March Farrakhan organized in Washington, D.C.

Tragedy continued to haunt Shabazz and her family. On June 1, 1997, Betty was severely burned as a result of a fire in her home in Yonkers, New York. She lingered in critical condition for three weeks before dying. Shabazz's twelve-year-old grandson, Malcolm Shabazz, Qubilah's son, was charged with setting the fire, reportedly because he was unhappy at being sent to live with his 61-year-old grandmother.

Malcolm X, though stung by this onslaught, responded calmly. "When you're involved in a revolution," he remarked, "nothing is painful." He set up his headquarters in Harlem's Theresa Hotel, where he preached the word of Allah and the gospel of political revolution, and he appeared at rallies, where he exhorted listeners to band together behind a unified militant movement and stand up to "the man," the ghetto

Malcolm X speaks at a rally in Harlem. His goal, he stated, was "the freedom of 22 million Afro-Americans by any means necessary."

term for whites. "You have to walk in with a hand grenade," he said, "and tell the man, 'Listen, you give us what we've got coming or nobody is going to get anything.'"

Malcolm X's split with the Nation freed him from its inflexible doctrines, and he widened his horizons. He developed an interest in orthodox Islam, or **Sunni Islam**, as practiced in the Middle East and Asia, and he began studying with Mahmoud Youssef Shawarbi, an Egyptian professor working in New York. He learned from Shawarbi that in the Islamic faith people were judged by their actions, not their color.

Shawarbi also guided his pupil toward a careful study of Islam's holy book, the **Qur'an**, whose scriptures caused Malcolm X to question many of his old assumptions.

Even before he had broken with the Nation, his conversations with Muslim students from North Africa and the Middle East—many of whom looked as "white" as any white American—had shaken his belief in the Nation's racial doctrines. These students did not quarrel with Malcolm X's political views, but they argued that his bitter denunciation of the white race did not square with Islamic teachings. Privately, he had begun to wonder if the students were right.

A PILGRIMAGE TO MECCA

Malcolm X's doubts about his own racial attitudes grew until he became deeply troubled. To help resolve his inner turmoil, he undertook an important mission: He went to Boston to visit his half-sister Ella, who had shocked him three years earlier by joining the Nation and then surprised him again by quitting the Nation and joining a more traditional Muslim group. Ella had stood by him throughout his trials, and now he had one more favor to ask of her: Would she lend him money for a pilgrimage to Mecca, the Islamic holy city?

All Muslims who are physically able are required to make at least one such pilgrimage, known as the **hajj**, to the holy city. Malcolm X's time had come at last, and Ella quickly agreed to sponsor his trip to the Saudi Arabian site. In April 1964, scarcely a month after announcing the formation of Muslim Mosque, Inc., he left quietly on his *hajj*. Only his wife and a few close aides knew where he was going. The pilgrimage was a personal matter he wanted kept out of the spotlight.

Mecca proved to be a revelation to Malcolm X. He marveled at the spirit of brotherhood and the sense of community in the holy city. He was greeted warmly by Muslims of every race and nationality on his visits to shrines and mosques and felt a strong kinship with them—not only with black Muslims from Africa but also with white-skinned, sandy-haired Eurasian pilgrims. The bitter differences between the races seemed to melt away under the warmth of shared religious faith.

RITUALS OF THE *HAJJ*

The *hajj*—the great pilgrimage to Mecca—is considered one of five major responsibilities of all Muslims. It takes place during the twelfth month of the Islamic lunar year, called Dhu-l-Hijjah. Each year, some two million pilgrims gather in Mecca at this time, spending the days in prayer, reading the Qur'an, and performing rituals. It is an opportunity for the pilgrims to renew their faith and to ask Allah to forgive their sins and transgressions.

The pilgrimage begins in Mecca, at an ancient cube-shaped building called the Ka'bah. (It is toward the Ka'bah that Muslims around the world are supposed to face when performing their daily prayers.) Wearing white clothing, the pilgrims circle the building seven times continuously in a counter-clockwise direction.

The most important event of the *hajj* takes place on the second day, on the Plain of Arafat, about 15 miles outside Mecca. Pilgrims must be there from noon to dusk. Most of them arrive in the morning, on foot or in buses and coaches. They encamp on the desert plain, creating a huge

---

Like all pilgrims, Malcolm X prayed in Mecca's Great Mosque and walked around the central symbol of Islam: the Ka'bah, with its sacred black stone. He also had a number of discussions with Islamic scholars and clergymen who wanted to know if any aspect of his pilgrimage had affected him. "The *brotherhood*!" he told them. "The people of all races, colors, from all over the world coming together as *one*! It has proved to me the power of the One God."

Malcolm X expanded on the effects of his *hajj* in an open letter to the press. "Never have I witnessed such sincere hospitality and overwhelming spirit of true tent city. In the middle of this plain stands the Mount of Mercy, where pilgrims pray to God for forgiveness of their sins. The spectacle of many thousands of people swarming over this hill, their hands and faces raised to God in prayer, makes Muslims think of the Last Day—the day when, they believe, the world will end and God will judge each individual soul.

On the third day of *hajj*, as the pilgrims travel back toward Mecca, they stop at the town of Mina. Here they throw seven small pebbles at each of three stone pillars. This ritual, called "stoning the Devil," is an expression of their rejection of evil and their determination to withstand temptation.

Later, the pilgrims remove their special clothes, wash themselves, and cut their hair to show that they are no longer in sin. They are now free to relax together and enjoy a festival that ends the *hajj*, called Eid al-Adha. The festival is held at Mina and begins with a big feast. Pilgrims must offer an animal for sacrifice, if they can afford it. If they cannot, they will share in the third of the meat set aside for the poor.

brotherhood as is practiced by people of all colors and races here in this ancient Holy Land," he wrote:

> For the past week, I have been utterly speechless and spellbound by the graciousness I see displayed all around me by people of all colors. . . . There were tens of thousands of pilgrims, from all over the world. They were of all colors, from blue-eyed blondes to black-skinned Africans. But we were all participating in the same ritual, displaying a spirit of unity and brotherhood

> Muslim pilgrims circle the Kaaba within the Great Mosque of Mecca, Saudi Arabia, during the *hajj*. Malcolm X was deeply moved by the spirit of harmony and understanding he found among people of all races during his pilgrimage to the holy city in the spring of 1864.

that my experiences in America had led me to believe never could exist between the white and non-white. . . .

You may be shocked by these words coming from me. But on this pilgrimage, what I have seen, and experienced, has forced me to rearrange much of my thought-patterns previously held, and to toss aside some of my previous conclusions. This was not too difficult for me. Despite my firm convictions, I have always been a man who tries to face facts, and to accept the reality of life as new experience and new knowledge unfolds it. I have always kept an open mind, which is necessary to the flexibility that must go hand in hand with every form of intelligent search for truth.

> During the past eleven days here in the Muslim world, I have eaten from the same plate, drunk from the same glass, and slept on the same rug—while praying to the same God— with fellow Muslims, whose eyes were the bluest of blue, whose hair was the blondest of blond, and whose skin was the whitest of white. And in the words and in the deeds of the white Muslims, I felt the same sincerity that I felt among the black African Muslims of Nigeria, Sudan, and Ghana.
>
> We were truly all the same—because their belief in one God had removed the white from their minds, the white from their behavior, and the white from their attitude. . . .
>
> Each hour here in the Holy Land enables me to have greater spiritual insights into what is happening in America between black and white. The American Negro never can be blamed for his racial animosities—he is only reacting to four hundred years of the conscious racism of the American whites. But as racism leads America up the suicide path, I do believe, from the experiences that I have had with them, that the whites of the younger generation, in the colleges and universities, will see the handwriting on the walls and many of them will turn to the spiritual path of truth—the only way left to America to ward off the disaster that racism inevitably must lead to.

Though Malcolm X promised that in the future he would judge people by their words and deeds, not by the color of their skin, his goal was still to organize black Americans for a revolt against white power. He was now willing to move swiftly and forcefully to the political center of the civil rights movement. He felt for the first time that, as he would later put it, "I can get along with white people who can get along with me."

Before leaving Mecca, Malcolm X celebrated his pilgrimage by taking an Islamic name, El-Hajj Malik El-Shabazz. He continued his spiritual journey by traveling to Lebanon and then to Africa, where many nations had recently gained their independence from European colonial powers. In Nigeria, students flocked to mass assemblies to hear the famed American activist speak, and they bestowed still another name on him: Alhadji Omowale Malcolm X. Omowale, which means "the child has come home" in the Nigerian language of Yoruba, was an apt name because he felt a strong bond with Africa. "I feel that I am at home," he told an audience in Ghana and added, "I'm from America, but I'm not an American."

Ghana's president, Kwame Nkrumah, entertained Malcolm X and then asked him to address the Ghanaian parliament. It was the ideal forum for Malcolm X. He had conceived of a broad new plan for linking the black African nations' struggle for political and economic independence with the struggle for justice waged by black Americans. He stated in his address that racism, poverty, and political oppression had common roots throughout the world, and that peoples of Third World nations—all of the underdeveloped countries on earth—must unite and guard against being economically exploited by powerful foreign nations and corporations. He called his new political philosophy "global black thinking."

The last stop on Malcolm X's journey was Algeria, which had recently won its independence from France. On May 19, 1964—his 39th birthday—he flew back to the United States. Much had changed in his brief absence. The country was in the throes of racial violence, even though civil rights groups had kicked off a new campaign with the hopeful phrase "Freedom Summer."

"Summer of Despair" was a more accurate term. In the South, black churches were firebombed, civil rights marchers were beaten by police, and the corpses of several activists were found in Mississippi fields. In the North, riots erupted in New York, Chicago, Philadelphia, and many smaller cities.

Malcolm X was prepared for this wave of racial disturbances. He drew up plans for a vast new movement that would promote black consciousness throughout the world. He met with a group of black radical thinkers and formed the Organization of Afro-American Unity (OAAU), a nonreligious branch of Muslim Mosque, Inc. Its

President Kwame Nkrumah of Ghana (pictured) invited Malcolm X to address his country's legislature. "[T]here is a growing tendency among black Americans today, who are able to see that they don't have freedom — they are reaching the point now where they are ready to tell the Man no matter what the odds are against them, no matter what the cost is, it's liberty or death," Malcolm told the audience. "If this is the land of the free, then give us some freedom. If this is the land of justice, then give us some justice. And if this is the land of equality, give us some equality.

program included traditional activist measures such as voter registration drives and school boycotts along with community projects aimed at improving urban housing and rehabilitating drug addicts.

Malcolm X also envisioned the OAAU as a black nationalist organization. Its agenda called for workers throughout the world to unite for the purpose of dismantling the capitalist economic system of private and corporate ownership of goods and property, on which most Western nations rested. He thus hoped to merge the black

Malcolm X was assassinated in 1965 during his weekly meeting with the Harlem community at the Audubon Ballroom, seen here in the aftermath of the shooting. (Chalk circles mark bullet holes in the rostrum where he was standing.) Although it was never confirmed, many suspected that the assassins were members of the Nation of Islam, upset by Malcolm X's challenge to Elijah Muhammad's authority and his disassociation from the organization.

power movement with socialism, an economic system in which goods and property are owned and controlled by the state.

So grand a mission required large funds—something Malcolm X sorely lacked—and he quickly set about raising money. In June 1964, he embarked on a busy schedule of speaking engagements and fund-raising rallies. He also launched a lobbying campaign at the United Nations, which he urged to pass a resolution condemning American racial policies.

In July, Malcolm X flew to Cairo, Egypt, where he addressed a group of representatives of African nations at a conference sponsored by the Organization of African Unity. The delegates treated their guest as if he were an official American ambassador and listened intently to his words. "Our problems are your problems," he told them. He then went on to argue that the struggle of black Americans paralleled the efforts of the emerging Third World nations.

After he gave his address, Malcolm X consulted with Islamic clergymen for ideas about expanding his ministry in America. He then took an extended tour of Africa. He was feted at several receptions given by heads of state, including his longtime hero Jomo Kenyatta, president of Kenya.

Malcolm X returned to the United States in November 1964, only to learn that the OAAU had foundered during his five-month absence. He immediately began another round of speaking engagements, hiring the Audubon Ballroom and other dance halls in Harlem for his meetings. He worked at a tremendous pace, often going without sleep and hardly seeing his family. As always, his speeches called for a full-scale black revolt against whites. "We must make them see that we are the enemy," he said. "Let them turn the money for defense in our direction and either destroy us or cure the conditions that brought us to this point."

THREATS AND CHALLENGES

As the year drew to a close, Malcolm X began to fear for his safety. Several of his aides had already been attacked and beaten by members of the Nation of Islam. A carload of his followers had been assaulted in a Boston tunnel and had averted trouble only because one of Malcolm X's men had produced a shotgun. Matters worsened in December, when Malcolm X himself received a series of death threats at both his home and office. Suddenly, he felt surrounded by enemies. Both the Nation and federal agents kept him under close surveillance, and he suspected a conspiracy was being organized against his life.

Yet Malcolm X did not back down. Instead, he kept up his public speaking campaign. The riots of the Freedom Summer led him to believe that his radicalism might win new converts among the SNCC and other student protest groups.

In February 1965, Malcolm X went to London, where he addressed an organization of African nations. From there he proceeded to Paris, where he planned to speak at a rally protesting U. S. involvement in the Vietnam War. Soon after his arrival, the French government deported him on the grounds that he was a security threat, and he lashed out at French officials for calling his presence "undesirable." Then rumors reached him that officials had discovered a plot to kill him in Paris and had deported him because they wanted to avoid an international incident on their soil.

More danger awaited Malcolm X upon his return to New York, including an incident that brought back frightening memories of his early childhood. It happened on the night of February 13, 1965. He and his family were asleep in their home in East Elmhurst when gasoline firebombs crashed through the picture window in their living room. He managed to herd his family out of the house just before flames engulfed half the building.

All along, Malcolm X had been certain that these attacks were the work of the Nation of Islam: His vocal criticism of Elijah Muhammad and his followers was being met with vengeance. He now began to wonder. Some of the incidents, especially the alleged plot in France, seemed beyond the capabilities of the Nation. He suspected that white supremacist groups and perhaps even the FBI had joined forces and were bent on intimidating him into silence.

He would not let them succeed. In fact, his message would soon reach more people than ever before with the publication of *The Autobiography of Malcolm X*. For several years, he had been dictating the story of his life to writer Alex Haley, and the work was almost completed. Malcolm X hoped the book would clarify public perception of his views and goals.

On Sunday, February 21, 1965, Malcolm X and his aides drove to the Audubon Ballroom for his regular weekly meeting with the Harlem community. The hall was about three-quarters full when, at 2:00 P.M., he stepped onto the stage to begin the meeting. He faced the audience and uttered a traditional Muslim greeting, "*As-Salaam-Alaikum*,

Scan here for news footage about Malcolm X's assassination:

brothers and sisters!" At that moment a man in the front row stood up, pulled out a sawed-off shotgun from his coat, and fired a shot into Malcolm X's chest. Two other men rushed forward and pumped more bullets into Malcolm X's body.

While the assailants fled the ballroom, Malcolm X's aides rushed to the side of their stricken leader. By the time he reached a hospital emergency room, the 39-year-old activist was dead.

One of Malcolm X's assassins, Talmadge Hayer, was captured outside the Audubon Ballroom, but his two accomplices—Norman Butler and Thomas Johnson—briefly escaped before being captured. The three were convicted of first-degree murder in March 1966. Police detectives suspected that the Nation was involved in the murder, but debate continues about precisely whether or not the three men had links to or were members of the Nation of Islam.

Some 1,500 people attended the funeral for Malcolm X, held in Harlem on February 27, 1965. After the funeral, friends took away the shovels from waiting gravediggers and instead buried Malcolm themselves, at the Ferncliff Cemetery in Hartsdale, New York. Later that year, his wife gave birth to their twin daughters.

CHAPTER 8: CHALLENGES AND THREATS   121

THE LEGACY

As the 1960s wore on, other public figures, among them Martin Luther King, Jr., fell to assassins' bullets. Violence ravaged more cities. Malcolm X's vision lived on through all the turbulence, all the sorrow, and all the death. Although Muslim Mosque, Inc., dissolved shortly after his demise, other voices, including those of the Black Panther movement founded by Huey Newton and Bobby Searle, echoed his call for sweeping changes in American society. The Black Panthers seized on Malcolm X's phrase "the ballot or the bullet" and used it as their slogan. The Nation of Islam remained at the forefront of the black separatist movement, eventually forgiving Malcolm X for his supposed transgressions and once more embracing him as one of its own.

Today, Malcolm X remains the best-remembered black militant of the 20th century. There was a resurgence of interest in his life in 1992, when director Spike Lee released his film *Malcolm X*. Nation of Islam leader Louis Farrakhan cited Malcolm's accomplishments and sacrifice in his speech before hundreds of thousands gathered in Washington, D. C. for the Million Man March in October 1995, echoing the words of Malcolm X when he told the huge crowd that white supremacy was the root of America's suffering.

At Malcolm X's funeral, actor Ossie Davis noted that, although the activist would be remembered for his controversial words, his legacy extended beyond rhetoric: "Here—at this final hour, Harlem has come to bid farewell to one of its brightest hopes—extinguished now, and gone from us forever… Many will ask what Harlem finds to honor in this stormy, controversial and bold young captain—and we will smile… We will answer and say unto them, 'Did you ever talk to Brother Malcolm? Did you ever really listen to him?… For if you did you would know him. And if you knew him you would know why we must honor him."

James Turner, the founding director of Africana Studies at Cornell University, experienced Malcolm X's passionate commitment to achieving true freedom for

A crowd is lined up to enter the Unity Funeral Home in Harlem, where a public viewing of Malcolm X was held. An estimated 15,000 people attended the viewing.

blacks. "This was a brother you could believe," Turner said. "There was the sense that he was not in it for something. That was the extraordinary thing about him. He was in it because of his commitment to our liberation."

At a time when Martin Luther King, Jr., was advocating peaceful resistance to achieve civil rights, Malcolm X's fiery arguments urging blacks to seize power through whatever means necessary represented a dramatic difference in the idea of how best to achieve social justice in America. Because Malcolm's positions moderated slightly near the end of his life, after his pilgrimage to Mecca, there is some thought that had both Malcolm X and Martin Luther King, Jr., lived longer, they might have discovered greater common ground in their views of the civil rights movement.

It is certain that Malcolm X placed a very different face on the struggle by people of color to achieve equality. It was often an angry face, a face that would not wait patiently for society to change but instead demanded respect and freedom *right now*. He spoke for a generation of young, politically active black people who felt betrayed by their country and, in some sense, by the slower pace of the civil rights movement.

Martin Luther King, Jr., understood this when he said, in a telegram to Betty Shabazz after her husband's assassination, "I always had a deep affection for Malcolm and felt that he had a great ability to put his finger on the existence and the root of the problem. He was an **eloquent** spokesman for his point of view and no one can honestly doubt that Malcolm had a great concern for the problems we face as a race."

One of America's most compelling public speakers, Malcolm X would not let his fight for racial justice be stopped—not by his white opponents, not by his enemies in the Nation, not even by an assassin's bullet. His powerful example of black activism continues to be felt throughout the world.

RESEARCH PROJECT

Using your school library or the internet, do research to answer the question, "Have race relations improved since the 1960s?" Present your answer to the class, using examples to support your conclusion.

TEXT-DEPENDENT QUESTIONS

1. What organization did Malcolm X found after leaving the Nation of Islam?
2. Who was Mahmoud Youssef Shawarbi?
3. What realization did Malcolm X have during the *hajj*?
4. What was the purpose of the Organization of Afro-American Unity (OAAU)?
5. What happened at the Audubon Ballroom on February 21, 1965?

RESOURCES

FURTHER READING

Burlingame, Jeff. *Malcolm X: Fighting for Human Rights*. Berkeley Heights, N.J.: Enslow, 2017.

Malcolm X. *Malcolm X Speaks.* George Breitman, ed. New York: Grove Press, 1994.

Malcolm X, with Alex Haley. *The Autobiography of Malcolm X.* New York: Ballantine, 1964.

Rickford, Russell John. *Betty Shabazz: A Remarkable Story of Survival and Faith Before and After Malcolm X.* Naplewood, Ill.: Sourcebooks, 2003.

Roberts, Randy, and John Matthew Smith. *Blood Brothers: The Fatal Friendship Between Muhammad Ali and Malcolm X.* New York: Basic Books, 2016.

Tinson, Christopher M. *Radical Intellect: Liberator Magazine and Black Activism in the 1960s.* Chapel Hill, N.C.: The University of North Carolina Press, 2017.

INTERNET RESOURCES

www.malcolmx.com
Malcolm X's official site, operated by his estate, includes a biography, facts, chronology of his life, and popular quotes.

www.brothermalcolm.net
This site contains scholarly research on Malcolm, his life, and activities.

www.columbia.edu/cu/ccbh/mxp/
The Malcolm X Project at Columbia University in New York is an ongoing effort to reconstruct the life of Malcolm X through multimedia resources and new historical research.

www.malcolm-x.org
This is a comprehensive site about the life and times of Malcolm X, including transcripts of his speeches and some discussion of the Islamic religion.

www.pbs.org/wgbh/amex/eyesontheprize
Based on the PBS American Experience television series *Eyes on the Prize: America's Civil Rights Movement 1954–1985*, this site links to profiles on people and documents from the time.

INDEX

A
Abyssinian Baptist Church, 44
Africa, 20, 91, 116, 119
Algeria, 116
Ali
    Muhammed, 104
    Noble Drew, 56
Allah, 54, 60
Amsterdam News, 88
Anger, 6–7
Apollo Theater, 37–38
Assassination, 95, 108–109, 118, 121
Atlanta, 81
Audubon Ballroom, 108, 118, 120
Autobiography of Malcolm X, The, 29, 120

B
Back to Africa movement, 21–22
Basie, Count, 30, 38
Bible, 59
Bimbi, 50
Birbeck College, 20
Birth, 17
Black Legion, 23–25
Black Muslims, 54, 71, 86–88, 99, 102
Black Panther, 122
Blood Brothers, 8–9
Boston, 27, 29–30, 32–36, 46, 78–80
    formation of temple, 78–79
Boycotts, 43–45, 84, 117
Burglary, 46
Butler, Norman, 121

C
Cairo, Egypt, 118
Capitalism, 117
Charlestown State Prison, 46–47, 49–51
Chicago, 77
Childhood, 17–19, 22–30
Children, 93, 109, 121
Cigarettes, 53–54
Civil disobedience, 85–86, 96
Civil rights, 7
    movement, contempt for, 84, 86, 99, 101
Civil Rights Act of 1964, 100–101

Civil War, 12, 18
Clay, Cassius, 104
Clothing, 34–36, 39, 41, 92
Colgate University, 44
Columbia University, 44
Concord, Massachusetts, 51
Congress, 45
    on Racial Equality (CORE), 84
Conk hairstyle, 36
Conscientious objector, 78
Cornell University, 122
"Cracking atoms," 83–84
Criminal acts, 28, 37, 39
Crisis, The, 67
Criticism of, 96–98

D
Dancing, 34
Davis, Ossie, 122
Death threats, 103–104, 119–120
Detroit, 62, 71
    Red, 40, 42
Dhu-I-Hijjah, 112
Draft board, 41, 77–78
Drinking, 34
Drugs, 34
    dealing, 40–42
Du Bois, W. E. B., 66–67

E
East Lansing, Michigan, 24–29
Economic Opportunity Act, 101
Eid al-Adha, 113
Ellington, Duke, 30, 38
Emotional condition, 41
Expelled, 28

F
Fard, E. W., 11
Fard, W. D., 55–59, 68, 73, 84
    teachings, 56
Farm, 24–25
Farrakhan, Louis, 94–96, 109, 122
Father. *See* Little, Earl
FBI, 120
Ferncliff Cemetery, 121
Fewclothes, 37
Firebombs, 120
"Fishing," 73–74
Fisk University, 66
Fitzgerald, Ella, 38
Force Bill, 19
Forty Thieves, 37, 39

France, 120
Freedom Summer, 116, 119
Fruit of Islam, 80, 83–88
Fund-raising, 118
Funeral, 121, 123

G
Gambling, 34, 46
Garvey, Marcus, 20–22, 25, 56
Ghana, 67, 116–117
Ghettos, 7
Gillespie, Dizzy, 37
Girlfriends, 35–36, 46
Global black thinking, 116
Goal, ultimate, 9
Gohannas family, 28
Gravitt, Joseph. *See* X, Joseph (Joseph Gravitt or Captain Joseph)
Great Depression, 23–25, 43
Great Mosque, 112, 114
Gun clubs, 8–9
Guns, 42, 46

H
Hajj, 111–114
Haley, Alex, 120
Harlem, 36–41, 81, 87, 108, 118, 121
    1964 race riots, 13–14
    Renaissance, 38
    1943 riots, 42–45
Hartford, Connecticut, 81
Hartsdale, New York, 121
Harvard, 66
"Hate That Hate Produced, The," 91
Hayer, Talmadge, 121
Holiday, Billie, 37
Hustling, 39–43

I
"I Have a Dream" (King), 100
Islam, 11, 13
    Sunni, 110

J
Jackson, Jesse, 95
Jazz, 30, 32, 34, 38
Jersey State College, 108
Jesus, 58
Jim Crow, 19–20
Johnson
    Hinton, 87
    Thomas, 121
Judiciary Committee, 45

Juvenile detention center, 29–30

K
Kaaba, 114
Ka'bah, 112
Kennedy
    International Airport, 7
    John F., 103
Kenya, 65
Kenyatta, Jomo, 65
King, Martin Luther, Jr., 9, 84, 96, 98, 122, 124
Korean War, 77
Ku Klux Klan, 16–19, 21–22, 54

L
Lansing, Michigan, 22–24
Lee, Spike, 122
Legacy, 122–123
Letter writing, 64
Liberation of blacks from white oppression, 9
Lincoln Memorial, 100
Lindbergh, Charles, 34
Lindy Hop, 34
Liston, Sonny, 104
Little
    Earl, 16–18, 20, 22–26
    Ella, 27, 29–30, 33, 36–37, 50, 111
    Hilda, 17, 26, 28, 53–54
    Louise, 17, 22, 26, 28
    Malcolm, 11
    Philbert, 17, 26, 53–54, 108
    Reginald, 26, 53–54, 68
    Robert, 26
    Wesley, 26
    Wilfred, 17, 26, 28, 70–71, 108
    Yvonne, 23, 26
Living Fountain assemblies, 84
Lobbying, 118
London, 120
Los Angeles, 81, 102
    confrontation, 99
Lynching, 19–20

M
Madhi, 57–58
Malcolm X, 122
Malcolm X Avenue, 95
Manner, 98
March on Washington, 99–101
Marijuana, 34, 37
Masjid Malcolm Shabazz. *See*

Temple Number Seven (Masjid Malcolm Shabazz)
Mecca, 11, 124
  pilgrimage to, 111–116
Medgar Evers College, 109
Mental hospital, 28
Message, 79, 96
"Message to the Grass Roots," 101
Messenger, The. *See* Muhammad, Elijah
Militant approach, 84, 86
Military segregation, 43
Million Man March, 95, 109, 122
Mina, 113
Moorish Temple of America, 56
Moses, 58
Mount of Mercy, 113
Muhammad, Elijah, 11, 54–60, 64, 66–68, 70, 72–73, 76–77, 79–80, 84, 91–92, 94, 99, 101, 103–104, 108, 118, 120
  studying with, 77
Muhammed Speaks, 92, 99
Muslim American Community, 94
Muslim Mosque, 107, 111, 116, 122
  reaction by Nation of Islam to, 108
Muslim Sisters, 83

N
Names, 11–12, 56
National Association for the Advancement of Colored People (NAACP), 67
National Mall, 100
Nation of Islam, 10–12, 53–60, 63–74, 76–88, 91, 99, 118–120, 122
  community, 73
  conversion to, 54–55, 60
  converts, drawing, 62, 81
  diet, 64
  drinking and smoking, 64
  mental, spiritual and moral discipline, 64
  national minister, 99
  recruits, 73–74
  rift with brother, 68, 70
  rift within, 101, 103–104, 107
  role of women, 83
  sex, 64

split in membership, 94
teachings, 56–59
  vs. traditional Islam, 11
Newton, Huey, 122
New York City, 8, 14, 81
  1964 shooting, 13
New York Police Department, 86–88
New York Stock Exchange, 25
Niagara Movement, 66
Nigeria, 116
Nkrumah, Kwame, 116–117
Norfolk
  Massachusetts, 51–55
  Prison Colony, 52, 63–68
Northern blacks, 22–23
Numbers runner, 45–46

O
Omaha, Nebraska, 17, 22
Organization of African Unity, 118–119
Organization of Afro-American Unity (OAAU), 116–118

P
Paris, 120
Parkhurst, Lewis, 52
Parole, 69–70
Pawn shops, 46
Peoples Voice, The, 45
Philadelphia, 81
  formation of temple, 79
Plain of Arafat, 112
Poole, Elijah. *See* Muhammad, Elijah
Pork, 53–54
Poverty, 26–27
Powell, Adam Clayton, Jr., 43–45
Prayer, 63, 112–113
Press conference May 21, 1964, 7, 9–10, 13
Prison preaching, 68
Prophet Muhammad, 11
Public speaking, 98

Q
Queens, 93, 97
Qur'an, 110, 112

R
Racism, 80
Reading program, 64–67
Reform school, 29–30
Rehabilitation, 52

Revolution, 9, 13, 90, 95–96, 107, 109
Reynolds, Georgia, 18
Robbery, 43
Roseland State Ballroom, 33–35
Roxbury, 30, 34, 46

S
Sammy the Pimp, 40
Sanders, Betty Dean. *See* X, Betty (Betty Shabazz)
Satan, 49
Savior's Day, 84, 86
Savoy Ballroom, 37–38
School, 26–29
  and prison, 50–53, 63–64
Searle, Bobby, 122
Segregation, 8, 18–19, 84
Self-defense, 9–10
Separatism, 20–22
Seventh Day Adventists, 26
Shabazz
  Betty. *See* X, Betty
  El-Hajj Malik, 115
  Malcolm, 109
  surname, 108
Shawarbi, Mahmoud Youssef, 110
Shorty, 33, 46
Slavery, 57, 59, 101
Small's Paradise, 37, 39
Socialism, 118
Solitary confinement, 49
Souls of Black Folk, The (Du Bois), 66
Southern Christian Leadership Conference (SCLC), 84
Springfield, Massachusetts, 81
Stoning the Devil, 113
Student Nonviolent Coordinating Committee (SNCC), 96, 119
Swerlins, 28–29

T
Temple Number
  One, 72, 74
  Seven (Masjid Malcolm Shabazz), 78, 81, 87, 92, 94
Tenements, 38
Theresa Hotel, 109
Turner, James, 122–123
Tuskegee Institute, 108

U
Unity, 97
Universal Negro Improvement Association (UNIA), 20, 22, 25, 54
University of Massachusetts, 108
"Up, You Mighty Race," 25

V
Vietnam War, 120
Vision, 68
Voter registration, 117

W
Wallace, Mike, 91
Washington
  Booker T., 67
  Dinah, 38
Welfare agents, 27–28
"We Shall Overcome," 101
West Indian Archie, 37, 46
"White Man's Heaven is a Black Man's Jail, A" (Farrakhan), 94, 96
White people, shift in approach to, 115
Whites, help with racism, 13
White supremacy, 17
Winston-Salem Teachers College, 94
Woodson, Carter G., 71
World War II, 36, 40, 43
Writing program, 63–64

X
Alhadje Omowale Malcolm, 116
Attilah, 93
Betty (Betty Shabazz), 91, 93, 108–109, 124
Cassius, 104
Gamilah, 93
Ilyasah, 93
Joseph (Joseph Gravitt or Captain Joseph), 82
Louis. *See* Farrakhan, Louis
Malaak, 93
Malikah, 93
Qubilah, 93, 109
significance of, 11–12

Y
Yacub, 58
Yankee Clipper train, 36–37

Z
Zoot suit, 34, 36, 41

ABOUT THE AUTHOR

Jillian Redmond is a freelance writer who lives in Hoboken, New Jersey. This is her first book.